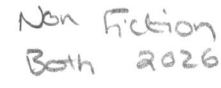

Kicking Against the Pricks

William Beckett

CONTENTS

DEDICATIONS   I

ACKNOWLEDGEMENTS   II

ABOUT THE AUTHOR   V

PREFACE   VI

INTRODUCTION   1

SO YOU WANT TO CHANGE THE WORLD?   7

ALL CHANGE!   19

SALES PEOPLE   29

OFFICES AND THEIR MEANINGS   48

MANAGERS – THE GOOD, THE BAD AND THE UGLY   61

MARKETING – WHEN THE RUBBER HITS THE ROAD   78

CONSULTANTS – WHO NEEDS THEM?   98

MANAGEMENT – SEEING THE WOOD FROM THE TREES?   109

MULTIMEDIA – ITS BIRTH AND MY PART IN IT   125

MILITARY MISSION – IN STEP AT LAST   143

VIRTUAL TRAVEL – DID YOU REALLY WANT TO GO THERE?   158

OMAN – THE LAST CRUSADE?   184

GARDENS – IS EVERYTHING IN THEM ROSY?   191

GOING TO THE MOVIES – IS THERE A CURE FOR CINEMANIA?   200

TRAVEL GUIDES – VIRTUALLY THERE?   205

EDUCATION – LESSONS LEARNED?   226

NATIONAL TRUST – ME I'M A DECENT SORT OF GUY...   232

THE GREAT POST OFFICE SWINDLE – REVEALED   238

SOFTWARE DEVELOPMENT – SMALL IS BEAUTIFUL   243

HEALTHCARE FOR THE AGED – FALLING FOR A DREAM   252

FUNDING – APPLY... OR DIE!?   282

ON CRAFTSMANSHIP – HOW DID YOU WANT TO SPEND YOUR LIFE?   295

FINALE & CREDO   301

AS THEY SAY IN YORKSHIRE, "THINK ON...."   316

MY MOTIVATION?   318

Dedications

It is with great honour that I dedicate this book to Virginia. Her constant support and resilience have been nothing short of amazing. Together, we faced and overcame countless trials and tribulations that come with standing up for what we believe is right. Her steadfastness is a testament to the strength of the human spirit. This book stands as a tribute to Virginia's courage and constant dedication.

Acknowledgements

A major and continuing influence on my life was the deputy headmaster of my first school, Mr. Toppin. He was the form master for the Fifth form and had been a top-class amateur footballer in the twenties and thirties with the famous Corinthian Casuals. He was amused by my being a fan of the great Arthur Bottom of York City, who was the hero of their FA Cup run to the Semi-Finals in 1954-55 when they were defeated by the eventual winners Newcastle United in a replay. For the first and only time at school I really put in some work, purely in order not to let Mr. Toppin down. When I joined the Army, Anthony Arkwright, my squadron leader, set a brilliant example, which I and his troop leaders endeavoured to follow. Rory Cochrane-Dyet was perhaps an even better leader and, fortunately for me, recommended me for the best job in the regiment as troop leader of the Reconnaissance Troop.

I owe a lot to Tom Bearley at Singer Business Machines, who encouraged and guided me and the rest of his sales team whilst maintaining a sense of humour when our expenses showed more inventiveness than usual. When I joined Arbat, I came under the influence of the splendid Doug Schilling, and he helped me get company approval for the software developments in communications systems that led to Arbat becoming, for a while, the pre-eminent supplier of computer systems in the City.

Nick Alexander at Virgin recruited me to develop and market some of the first multimedia products and was invariably encouraging and supportive, with a great sense of humour which enlivened every meeting. Jon Baldachin came up with the idea of producing a multimedia version of Cluedo and helped get the project underway. This led to the formation of Armchair Travel, which I founded with William Donelson in the early 1990s. Thanks to William's brilliance in the software field, we survived for more years than could have been anticipated at the start, and he brought in Rickie Gauld, a marvellous lighting cameraman who filmed all our projects and became a real friend. Jeremy Westwood, managing director of Insight Guides, the only honest publisher that I had dealings with, became a great friend and purveyor of excellent advice.

When I started Hip Impact Protection in 2009, I was helped enormously by my old friend, Lavinia Aykroyd, and her husband, David, who introduced me to Crispin Odey, the hedge fund entrepreneur. Together with Nicholas Lambarde-Scott, a friend and tennis opponent from Nottinghamshire, and David Fisher, for whom my wife Virginia had done much interior decorating work, they invested in and supported HIP through some very difficult times.

Last, but not least, my half-sister Clare's daughter-in-law, Frances Crewdson, has been a great help and supporter in recent years.

As well as Virginia, my family, who are too numerous to mention individually, have been a great source of strength, and even when they were clearly somewhat dumbfounded by my approach to life and business, they have never ventured any criticisms – at least to my face or knowledge – and have all been enormous fun whenever we meet. What more could one ask?

About the Author

William Beckett is a very experienced entrepreneur who has tried for 50 years to change the world with innovative hi-tech products that tackled major problems in education, industry, entertainment, healthcare, communications and the City of London. His relatively poor education and a spell in the Army taught him that the only important thing is to stand up for yourself, especially if you are right!

Preface

I have a vision of what the future holds for me. On arrival at the Pearly Gates, St. Peter asks the usual questions, "Full name? First line of address and Postcode? Date of Birth? First and third digits of your PIN number? Mother's maiden name?" As I answer these, I see his assistant is entering the details on a PC and ask why, for heaven's sake, he is using Microsoft Windows?

St. Peter replies, "I'm not really into technology but we had this consultant that recommended it – mind you, he will now be spending a few aeons in Purgatory!"

Emboldened by this, I then ask St. Peter about the Pearly Gates, as they look to me like a rather skew-whiff design. "Milord Rogers is responsible for them" he replies, "but we have arranged for him to live in a building he himself designed – and I hear he is complaining a bit." Then he says sternly, "But that's quite enough criticism from you, Beckett, you're for the drop too now."

"Oh no," I plead, "An eternity with Bill Gates, I can't stand it."

"No." says St. Peter with a wry smile, "We have reserved a special place in hell for Mr. Gates. He's destined to use Windows Vista for a few millennia – quite appropriate, don't you think, after foisting the Millennium Bug on us? Though I do hear that even a few hours with Vista feels like forever."

He then adds, "For you, Mr Beckett, we have reserved a conference room in Purgatory for endless meetings with lawyers – of which you'll find plenty down there – though you **are** allowed, even encouraged, to kick one or other of them under the table from time to time!"

"It is hard for thee to kick against the pricks".

- Holy Bible, Acts ix. 5

Introduction

Business books are usually written for and about the large corporate sector. However, there are millions of people managing and working in small businesses all over this country, as in others, so it is arguably a more important sector than its larger cousin. Certainly, most product and service innovations, as well as new ideas, come from small businesses. But small businesses have to deal with big business, and therein lies their problem, because, with a few heroic exceptions, Big does not care how badly or unethically it behaves. I believe it is time to describe the experiences of running a small business for 30

thinks, "Surely he can't be that BIG"

years and, by-the-bye, taking on the big corporations so that you will have been warned about what will happen when you start a new business, particularly in the high-tech arena. Or, if you are already in business for yourself, maybe this book will resonate with you, as it often feels pretty lonely running a Small.

How do you define a small business? Most people would consider that an organisation with more than 150 people is no longer a small business; in fact, Gore Associates, the inventor and manufacturer of Goretex, opens a new office or manufacturing facility when one of its business units gets bigger than about 150-160 people and does this because it recognises that no one person can know each other person, and maintain a relationship with, a circle of more than around 150 people. It is instructive that Gore "never thought of success in purely financial terms, they think of success in terms of making useful things and having fun doing it." This echoes the words of Robert Townsend, author of "Up the Organisation", the most acute, and probably the funniest, book ever written about business still in print, who almost 50 years ago wrote, "If you don't do it excellently, don't do it at all, because if it's not excellent it won't be profitable or fun, and if you're not in business for fun or profit, what the hell are you doing there?" He also observed that excellence and size are fundamentally incompatible.

So the message is that having fun is important and that small is better – even if you are actually rather large – Gore has 13,000 people in scores of facilities, but not a single manager; all their people are called "associates" – does anyone like the idea of being 'managed'? But, as Gore has proved over the past 60+ years with a steady stream of new products, to survive, it is essential to keep innovating. Bigs always find it cheaper to go on producing more of the same rather than close down a production line and switch it to a new process or product, so even if one of their people does invent something new, it frequently does not get out of **their** door. More often than not, the frustrated innovator leaves and forms his or her own company to exploit it – so the Big loses twice over.

Introduction

This is not the time nor place to trace in detail the history of computing, but it might be helpful for those who were not present at that time to observe its development to mention some of the key elements as it expanded rapidly from a relatively small number of computer centres owned by private corporations and Government departments in the 1960s to the plethora of computing devices of all shapes and sizes common today. The market in the 60s was dominated by IBM (Snow White) with its massive – at least in physical footprint – 360 and 370 mainframe machines, though the other Seven (Dwarves) mainframe computer companies also featured – Burroughs, Univac, NCR, Control Data, Honeywell – with RCA and General Electric disappearing/merging by 1971 – and the British ICL favoured by the UK Government (bringing up the rear). However, emerging from the industrial control market were a number of upstart mini-computer companies like Digital Equipment Corporation (DEC), Data General and Hewlett-Packard in the USA that typically manufactured 16-bit machines and featured a wide variety of interfaces typically required to control industrial machinery. In business applications, their software shared the use of the processor between a number of concurrent tasks, such as input from Visual Display Unit (VDUs) terminals and output to printers.

The software, as always, was the problem since industry required a very different set of programs to banking, accounting organisations, etc., so consequently, there was an opportunity for companies like Arbat in the City of London to develop and sell not

3

only the required real-time foreign exchange and banking applications, but also to optimise the minicomputer's Operating System for such operations using Unix as the base, which had been licensed from Bell Labs or, if it suited, the version from University of Berkeley, California. The applications for these machines could then be programmed in BASIC which was a relatively easy language to learn and use. This happened in the early to mid-1970s, and by the end of the decade, it was becoming possible to closely network machines to enable them to work together to do the heavy end-of-day processing, for example, or for a back-up machine to automatically take over if a part of one system failed, which was not unusual in those days, a time when all these systems demanded climate-controlled computer rooms to operate efficiently.

In about 1974, George Cogar produced the first 8-bit microcomputer in a small desktop unit with an integrated keyboard, small screen, processor, 8K memory, double mini-tape storage and communications interface to IBM or other computers; indeed, these devices were marketed initially as 'intelligent terminals'. DataPoint produced a competitive machine with similar facilities but using floppy discs rather than tapes. These machines and a central hard disc-based storage system could be linked together with co-axial cable to produce the first distributed processing systems, and their great virtue was that individual independently programmed workstations could be placed where the work was, not in an expensive purpose-built computer room. Since each workstation had its own processor and memory, it was not dependent on borrowing processing power from a central unit, as with minicomputer and mainframe systems.

When Apple Computer came out with the Apple II in 1977, it was the first readily available 8-bit home computer that could actually handle spreadsheets and word processing, though in rather limited forms. It was copied by the likes of Commodore with its Amiga for games and Acorn with the BBC machine oriented towards education in the late 1970s/early 1980s. They soon featured colour screens, or in some cases TVs, and used floppy discs and/or tape cassettes for program loading and data storage.

Multimedia only really became feasible with the use of Personal Computer-controlled laser videodiscs in the early 1980s, but this approach was rather cumbersome and expensive at around £5,000 a unit, so only found a niche in industrial training where the potential pay-off in accident prevention or improved output quality of industrial production would warrant such expenditure. It was only with the advent of CD-ROM (for holding the programs and data) and much-improved processors and screens with the Apple Macintosh and later versions of the IBM PC that proper multimedia with colour images, video, sound and graphics became feasible and economic enough in the 1990s that it was worth making exciting programs that could be widely published for a new and emerging market. There was then an all-too-brief honeymoon period for CD-

ROM in the mid-1990s before it too was superseded by the Internet and in due course, smartphones from 2000 onwards. Selling a physical entity like a CD-ROM was feasible, but asking people to pay for access to a website with the same content was never a starter. We did find ways of adopting the advertising model on our websites to generate revenue but never had the clout of a major player like Google to really exploit that approach.

Apart from mainframes, I designed, developed and marketed scores of products for all these types of machines over many years and in all respects, it was very satisfying to see the results of one's labours making life more worthwhile and sometimes safer, but in many cases more interesting and entertaining, for people of all ages and in many walks of life. Whether that qualifies as 'changing the world,' I am not sure, but if I, with my colleagues, were responsible in many of these fields for leading or accelerating positive change using new technology, even though it might well have happened later on, that is not such a bad epitaph.

So You Want to Change the World?

Well, do you? People pontificate about the work/life balance as if it was something that had only occurred in the 21st century and specifically only to them, whereas it has been an issue since the caveman wondered whether he should chase the woolly mammoth for sport and food, or stay in the mouth of the cave with his wife and children in case the sabre-tooth tiger happened by. The real balance is the choice between settling for the world as it is or trying to make a difference. Are you happy to leave to others the struggle to improve things, or do you believe that we were put on this earth to change the way the world works – for the better? Can you pass up an opportunity to try to make the system better when you see just how badly most things work? Do you believe in continuous improvement of the process? According to George Bernard Shaw, "The reasonable man adapts himself to the world; the unreasonable one persists in trying to adapt the world to himself. Therefore, all progress depends on the unreasonable man."

If you want to make it a better world, not just a more comfortable one for you and your family, it is probably going to be a struggle, and however brilliant you are, the opposition you will encounter will amaze you, especially from those you would think would be on your side. Famously, the new Member of Parliament said that he was looking forward to taking on the 'enemy' party sitting opposite, to be told by an older and wiser MP that the 'enemy' was sitting behind and around him, not amongst the party opposite! Make no mistake; the *settlers* will try to get you once they realise you are a *seeker* because the last thing that settlers want is a seeker after truth, upturning their world. Big corporations are almost invariably full to the brim with settlers, and if you happen to work for a Big – which most people do in their formative and most intellectually dynamic years – settlers will do their level best to thwart your brilliant scheme – whatever it is.

You don't believe me? Look at the struggle that (Sir) Frank Whittle had in getting the jet engine accepted – an Air Ministry official described it as "impracticable" – even in the years (1930s) of his country's greatest and most desperate need. Check out the story of the gunnery range table (the world's first electrically powered mechanical analogue computer) that was invented and perfected by Arthur Pollen but not fitted to British ships in the First World War; a greatly inferior system developed by the Navy itself being preferred. This resulted in the poor gunnery, which lost the battle of Gallipoli, and also at Jutland which let the German battle fleet escape and almost lost Britain the war. Both are examples of the inventor coming from left field – Whittle was an RAF officer, and Pollen a writer on naval affairs.

As my ancestor, Edmund Beckett-Denison, the gifted amateur horologist, wrote 130 years ago, after the struggle he had had with officialdom in getting Big Ben with its clock and tower, designed, built and installed, "The tendency of the official mind to get things done with as little trouble as possible is infinitely stronger than to get them done as **well** as possible. I was only brought into this business originally with a view of saving someone else trouble; as soon as it was found that by the legal effect of the contract, I had real power to direct the work, every possible effort was made to get rid of it, and me. No official who joined in those attempts cared three half-pence how the clock was made. Luckily, I did care and knew what would become of it if I gave up." The clock is still going. Incidentally, Tony Benn, the veteran Labour MP, made similar comments about the Civil Service when he was a minister in the 1970s, so not much has changed.

All of these inventors took the view that better technology could make a real difference, and of course, since the 1950s, computers have been touted as an agent of change; however, to the delight of the Luddites, they have frequently been misapplied, just as a hammer can break things as well as make them. In fact, it is at least questionable whether computers (as opposed to computer chips incorporated in other devices) have improved efficiency and reduced production costs overall, given fiascos such as the "millennium bug", which cost the world economy at least $30 billion, the vast amount of pointless web surfing, spam e-mails, phishing, viruses and so on. It has been claimed that the millennium bug did not actually exist and was a figment of the consultants' imagination, but this is wrong in that the vast majority of PCs installed in business were still running Windows 95 in 1999/2000, as Windows 97 only came out just before the millennium, and they had not yet been converted to it.

"Great! I'll order 5,000 of them!"

My company, Armchair Travel, had a machine running Windows 95, luckily not with mission-critical applications, and when we restarted it after the New Year on January 2nd 2000, we had terrible problems and had to do endless re-loads of software and applications. What did Microsoft think they were doing releasing an operating system (Windows 95), which was launched – late – in 1997 when, just three years later, it would have to cope, as they must have known, with the millennium date change? After all, the advent of the year 2000 was hardly a surprise as it could have been confidently and accurately predicted hundreds, even thousands of years ago. Either this is sheer incompetence, or was it a bung to the consultants, who were thus able to charge £billions to fix the problem? After all, lazy consultants, as we shall see, nearly always recommend the predominant market supplier, ergo a quid pro quo?

Perhaps the use of computers to enable office workers to work from home will eventually prove to be the machines' greatest benefit – what could be more counter-productive than making millions of people commute every weekday into the world's great cities to sit at a desk on a piece of real estate that costs up to £700 per square foot per year, equating to about £135,000 a year for the average footage needed per person. It may be argued that it is vital for people to come into the office, but given the amount of in-fighting, time-wasting and pointless meetings mainly called for the purpose of management self-aggrandisement, it is certainly doubtful if offices actually improve productivity.

This obviously does not apply to manufacturing and (most) research establishments. Better communication techniques, such as video conferencing, document work-sharing, etc., should enable most of the present in-office communication to be delivered more cheaply and efficiently without requiring workers to exhaust themselves, travelling crushed together for an hour or two every day into the city. Post-lockdown office attendance in the capital is at about 60 per cent of pre-pandemic levels, and office workers in central London come into work 2.3 days a week on average.

Personal experience bears out the settler theory. Working at a small (less than 100 people) software systems house called Arbat in the City in the late 1970s, I was encouraged by their technical director, the brilliant Douglas Schilling, to devise, design, market and sell the world's first commercial e-mail system, a development from Arbat's successful automatic telex handling and telegraphic message-switching or store-and-forward switching system, as it is sometimes known, system.

After it had been developed and tested, it was decided that, with the help of the company's PR agents, a Press Conference should be called, at which the company's founder and chairman, John Atkinson, would announce the release of the first commercial electronic mail system, which I then demonstrated. After the meeting, all hell broke loose. The managing director said that the release had not been authorised by him or the board, and he demanded that the PR people be requested to gainsay the release and contact the attendees from the Press to kill the story.

Why did he and the board do this? Basically, it came down to fear that I and Doug Schilling were dragging the company in a direction that he did not want it to go. He and the other directors were comfortable with the banking systems and customers that he had been dealing with for many years, and the thought of launching into a new market area unfamiliar to them was, frankly, terrifying.

What he did not know, because he had never asked, was that the message-switching system (using telegraph lines and telex) already contained all the necessary code to become an electronic mail system, and it was merely waiting to be activated at the numerous sites where the message switches had already been installed. In fact, some months later, after I had left the company, Shell and other customers of the message switch, previously alerted by me, requested that the e-mail system be activated. It took less than a morning for the company's chief software engineer on the system to implement the full e-mail in-house system – pretty similar to those we all use now, albeit over the Internet – which did not exist then.

Actually, the company situation was even worse than that because, after the abortive Press launch, a role was soon 'found' for Doug Schilling in Hong Kong, where the company had a couple of customers, and the company's chairman found himself in New York with no further active role in the management or direction of the company. The board apparently took the view that e-mail systems would never take off as a concept, and all the work to develop the first one and market it to a sector that had a desperate need for it and the money to

pay for it was completely pointless – much safer to stay with banking systems, obviously. In fact, all the company's communication systems products, which also included a SWIFT interface system for banks, allowing a completely integrated banking and communication systems approach, were killed off a year or two afterwards by the company's decision to move away from its own Unix-based operating system and run its banking application software under the Digital Equipment Corporation's 32-bit VAX operating system – VMS.

It was impossible to run any of the communication systems on VMS and the company's decisive advantage over IBM and others disappeared almost overnight, with the result that sales of the banking system soon dried up also. This was a particularly short-sighted decision as it actually **was** possible to run Unix on VAX machines, and so, with some modification, the e-mail system could have been made to work. As Thomas Watson of IBM said, "Once an organisation loses its spirit of pioneering and rests on its early work, its progress stops."

Several years later, I met the sales manager of IBM's City branch, Martin Knight, who had been responsible for sales to banks at that time, and he told me that Arbat had completely wiped the floor with IBM and that he could not understand why the company had suddenly disappeared. After their sales had dried up, Arbat was sold for quite a lot of money to Control Data, a mainframe supercomputer company, and then on to a Swiss banking system specialist. Both of these companies soon faded away.

Are there any lessons to be drawn from this fiasco? The *settlers* in Arbat were doubtless delighted that they had slapped down the upstart communications systems division, but in reality, they had forgotten the two golden rules: firstly, that it is absolutely necessary to maintain any competitive advantage that you already have, and second, that if a new opportunity, such as e-mail, opens up that you can exploit at virtually zero additional cost, you must grasp it, or be condemned to anonymity.

Would an internal e-mail system at such an early date, ie the early 1980s, have been accepted before the arrival of the Internet? The reason that Shell wanted it was because their 100-terminal network jammed up with incoming messages from their North Sea platforms if they were printed centrally at their HQ in Aberdeen – and then manually walked round the offices to the addressees – and that the responses to them did not get out quickly enough if they were also typed in at a central point in the Aberdeen office.

The solution was to distribute terminals and printers around the Aberdeen offices and, route the messages directly to the addressees, and supply them with terminals to enable them to reply. The system utilisation improved enormously so messages got delivered and replied to much more quickly, with the workflow in the office being completely streamlined and no more messengers scurrying about. The savings were more than enough to pay for the system. Obviously this technique could have been applied, albeit on low-speed telex and telegraph lines, to many other large organisations with a significant number of departments and outlying offices, even though there was not then a public service network like the Internet. Nowadays, there must be very few big companies or large offices – if any – without their own Intranet.

Incidentally, Arbat did try to connect their system to what was, at that time in the late '70s, called the ARPANET, the predecessor to the Internet, which then consisted of less than half a dozen nodes, mostly at universities and research institutions, but unfortunately, the node we connected to was not using the published packet switching protocol, and our system crashed that node and then the others, with the result that we were banned from ever connecting again.

The system at Shell was manned day and night, and in fact, if a rig turned over (as happened with Piper Alpha), there was a standing instruction to insert a tape loop with an SOS on it into the teleprinter on the rig linked to our system. Naturally, the operators in Aberdeen got bored during the night, and one of them remembered that Arbat had used some 'hangman' and 'dungeons and dragons' text games to teach the operators the use and features of the VDU terminals. She got going on these games together with her friends in the operators' room, and we had a call a few days later to ask why our system ran so slowly in the night that messages were taking hours to be delivered. We examined the system logs and discovered that almost all the CPU power was being used by the gamesters! The games were removed immediately.

When we were installing the system at Shell, I was shown the computer room and asked my advice on positioning our system. I asked where they were thinking of putting it and noticed there was a huge silver foil-covered tube in the ceiling directly above that. I immediately suggested another location, and luckily, they implemented my advice because a few weeks later, with the system running at full blast, the very same pipe split, unleashing a torrent of water which would have wrecked the computers.

It took a sea change for British manufacturing to subscribe to the concept of continuous improvement of process. In the 1980s, it had become apparent that quality control at British companies lagged far behind that of the Japanese, Germans and the Americans, with the result that products manufactured in the UK, such as cars, were being turned out with appalling records of reliability, for example, Jaguar which was – apart from the Rolls-Royce – the flagship of the British motor industry at that time. Captains of industry, such as Sir John Egan, then chief executive of Jaguar Cars, mouthed their belief in quality control without actually implementing it on the shop floor.

The result was that Jaguar had to provide longer and longer warranties so that their customers were not financially disadvantaged when their cars did not work properly. The costs of this took Jaguar to the verge of bankruptcy and, at the end of the decade, caused the firm to be bought out by Ford, a firm that did already subscribe to Statistical Process Control. I will return to SPC later, but the point is that change is not a to-be-dreaded one-off event.

Managing change effectively and continuously is a necessary component of remaining in business, so unless we embrace change and, indeed, actively seek it out, we are heading, sooner or later, for business oblivion. Remember that (almost) no business idea is good forever. Still happy to be a settler? It may be an easier life... until you experience a "Black Swan" event, but when that happens – game over.

All Change!

One would have thought that the computer and communications business would be among the most open in the world in embracing change, and I suppose that compared to some other industries, like publishing, this could be true, however, people's mindset is pretty much the same whatever industry they are in. I remember asking a sales guy who worked for me if he was interested in the future of technology, only to receive the amazing reply that no, he wasn't, particularly. Given that this was a very smart guy, working in a very hi-tech field, I was absolutely astonished by his attitude, and when I asked why, he replied that the future would come along soon enough whatever he did. Several people at the same company overheard this conversation and expressed no surprise or dissent.

The company we all worked for then, in the mid-1980s, was Nixdorf Computer, which was at that time one of the leading computer companies in the world and probably the top indigenous computer company in Europe. It had been extraordinarily successful in the mini-computer field with a range of 16-bit minis and terminals especially adapted for banks and supermarkets, and with a range of small business systems. It had also developed copies of IBM mainframes, word processing systems, data entry systems, all sorts of other devices and even private telephone exchanges, most of which were sold very successfully in Germany. But, apart from the banking and supermarket systems, none of the others had really succeeded outside Germany because they were exposed to much stronger competition in other countries, especially the US, and were seen as not particularly cutting edge, and frequently rather expensive, due to tariffs, exchange rates, shipping costs and so on.

Nixdorf Computer, like other mini-computer manufacturers, such as Digital Equipment Corporation (DEC), had a problem. Users were demanding more power at the work desk so that each "dumb" workstation could undertake more tasks more flexibly without "borrowing" central processing power from the small 16-bit minicomputer controlling all the terminals in that office. If all the terminals were doing much the same task at the same time, as in a bank or supermarket, it was not too much of a problem for the mini.

However, this was becoming less and less often the case, and it was clear that new customers for the system were beginning to look elsewhere. Nixdorf responded by buying portable PCs from Panasonic, but these were just standard machines with spreadsheet and word processing applications, not at all suited to the more demanding specialist environments 'enjoyed' by Nixdorf's customers. Obviously, Nixdorf looked at high-speed broadband cable networks to link their minis but, like DEC, did not embrace networked "intelligent workstations", such as SUN (Stanford University Network) using UNIX, because that would have required a complete re-write of their software and a complete re-think of their marketing. By the late 1980s, Heinz Nixdorf, the charismatic and dynamic figure who had founded the company, had died and left his company in the hands of two marketing men, who, if they did agree on a strategy, failed to implement it. One of them, Arno Bohn, eventually left and moved on to head up Porsche, where he nearly buried that company, too.

In fact, it had been pretty obvious since the mid-1970s that what were then known as "intelligent terminals" would supersede "dumb" workstations sooner or later. The amazingly creative former Univac engineer and inventor, George Cogar, had designed and built the first of these systems in the early 1970s and they had enjoyed some success after Singer Business Machines took over Cogar's company in 1974. The terminals could be linked together by co-axial cable, which allowed a network of workstations to be set up, each controlling its own devices, such as printers, and capable also of connecting to mainframes etc.

This system was the forerunner to the Apollo and Sun workstations of the 1980s and was further developed by ICL after it took over Singer Business Machines in 1976. However, Nixdorf was not alone; DEC killed off the PRISM (later Alpha) architecture in 1988 because they did not want it to compete with their VAX systems, only to realise somewhat belatedly in 1992 that the simplified RISC architecture of the Alpha, when built into a workstation, completely outperformed the VAX large mini-computer system, housed in a computer room. But by then, it was too late for DEC, which was eventually sold to Compaq in 1998. In fact, it took the resignation and retirement of Ken Olsen, who had started DEC in 1957 and masterminded the world-wide pre-eminence of its minicomputer systems, to effect the change. Olsen had famously pontificated in 1977 – after the emergence of the Apple II – that he saw no reason for anyone to have a computer in their home!

The common factor in these disasters is that the extraordinary success that these companies achieved in their fields led directly to their ultimate failure. Their directors appeared to believe that they walked on water and that by willing something to be so, it would be. They were unwilling to risk their personal credibility and their companies' huge profits to effect change before they absolutely had to, and by then, it was usually too late.

It is always easier and more profitable to 'settle' into producing more of the same than to 'seek' out and meet new challenges. A good example of this mindset is the hubristic remark attributed to the Chief Executive of NCR, who, when asked in the mid-1970s if he proposed to move into the new field of Point-of-Sale systems, pointed out of the window at the tall factory chimney and said, "While there is smoke coming out of that chimney, we will continue to make cash registers". NCR cash registers, the name brand in the market, were swept aside by Point-of-Sale systems, pioneered by

Singer Business Machines, later ICL/Fujitsu, and others, in the 1980s.

However, too much change can also be bad for your company's health. In 1970, a visionary engineer called Campbell, who, as chief executive, launched an initiative at Singer Business Machines to release a new product, or system, *every* month. That might have been reasonable if the products were developments of existing lines, but almost all of them took the company into completely new fields against strongly entrenched market competitors. For example, the System Ten, a small business computer competing with IBM's System 3; an accounting system with magnetic stripe cards that competed with NCR; a Point-of-Sale system that competed with NCR's cash registers; probably the earliest phototypesetting machine, competing with Monotype and Linotype hot-metal systems; a photocopier that competed with Xerox; a data entry system competing with Mohawk and others, and so on for a full twelve months!

Naturally, the people at Singer, though very excited by the rush of new products, suffered severe product indigestion and took a year or two to get some sort of handle on the sales product knowledge and the support required. In fact, many of the systems were competitive in price, with much better specifications and frequently superior technology to their competitors, though really it would have been enough to just launch the System Ten with its POS and Factory

Control system peripherals and concentrate on training the sales force and building up the support services required.

Change is not always for the better. Since World War II, Friden had been supplying paper tape-based automatic writing machines which allowed standard letters and documents to be produced (originally as individually printed standard letters informing next-of-kin of the death of a serviceman and at the same time punching a paper tape in telex form so that a telegram could be sent off immediately) and printed at about 10-12 characters a second, and the company had pretty well achieved a monopoly of the market.

However, with the advent of the IBM golf ball typewriter in the late 1960s, a number of companies linked the golf ball printer to paper tape readers and punches to achieve a slightly faster printing speed at lower noise levels than the Friden machine (which used metal type bars), could manage. The new machines rapidly took Friden's market until it became apparent that the golf ball head, which was made for lightness from plastic with a metal coating, could not cope with the continuous printing required from an automatic machine, as opposed to the typist speeds it was designed for. Friden machines duly re-took this market. This unreliability was well known to the British Government, so Friden, for a couple of years, supplied 95% of the market for these devices to Government departments. I was that lucky salesman.

At about this time, the government went out to tender for some 1,000 terminals for the DHSS offices around the country that would read, in this case, printed edge-punched cards with details of social security benefit claimants, print a document with new data input, e.g. amount and date, and transmit the details to their central computer. Friden got a contract to supply the devices that produced the printed edge-punched cards and warned the DHSS in writing that the terminals they were favouring would be unreliable, which indeed proved to be the case.

What Friden, and in this case I, should have done was to refuse to supply the edge-punched card devices, unless we also supplied the terminals, all on a single tender. Unfortunately, I had just taken over the Government business, so did not know the background of the tender and was only too happy to get a small order, but I totally missed the point that the mass terminal system would not work without the unique devices we supplied that drove them.

I did, however, learn the lesson that, in some cases, the best strategy is to threaten to walk away if you are in a strong enough position. For example, some years later I was invited to tender for a large message-switching system by BP in competition with their own systems company called Scicon. I knew that Scicon did not really have a product but that, nevertheless we would be certain to be beaten up by them during the tendering process. I, therefore, stopped the sales guy who worked for me from responding to BP's invitation until after the tender deadline had passed.

Naturally, he and my senior management got the screaming willies about this, and it was made pretty clear that my days were numbered if my approach lost us the order. At the end of the day, when the tender was due, I got a call from BP asking why we had not submitted a tender, to which I replied that we had assumed that Scicon would be given the deal. BP told us that it would be greatly to our advantage to submit a tender if we could do so in the next few days. No problem and we got a large order for several systems at the full price of about £1 million.

Carl Friden had invented the first electrically-powered automatic calculator in the early 1930s in Oakland near San Francisco and needed to show the early prototype to potential investors from the American Box Company, which dealt in wood and had no idea about calculating machines. He took the ferry across from Oakland (the Bay Bridge was not yet built) and presented the machine in the hushed boardroom of American Box, where it sounded like a machine gun.

Sent away with his tail between his legs, he pondered the problem while going back on the ferry and realising that the ball bearings were the cause of the noise, he removed them and returned on the next ferry back to San Francisco and the AB boardroom, where the board meeting was still going on. He now re-performed the calculations he had done earlier but with the display facing him.

Naturally, the machine was now almost silent as the numbers whizzed past the display window at random! He got his investment. Carl Friden was well-known as an honourable man, a remarkable inventor – he also designed many of the machine tools for the production line that produced the calculators – and an excellent employer and must have known when he undertook this somewhat desperate measure, that given time he could deliver a quieter production machine, which would, in any case, be used in the relatively noisy hubbub of a busy office.

At Singer in 1974, I was asked to supply an intelligent terminal for the Foreign Office, which would have the task of communicating with a mainframe computer at Norwich which held details of the VIPs, such as ambassadors, and their place in the order of protocol – basically who was senior to whom, but more importantly, who should on no account sit next to whom at formal dinners, or be asked to the same cocktail party – apparently there had been a disastrous incident sometime before. The Foreign Office also wanted the device to perform a basic text editing and replacement function, then store and recall the text, which, along with good quality printing using a daisy wheel printer[1] once we had programmed it to do these

---

1 A circular plastic wheel with individual 'petals' with an alpha, numeric or symbol character on the end of each. It rotated at high speed and a hammer struck

things, was, I suppose, the very first word processing system installed in the UK, and probably one of the first in the world. I was really nervous about getting the intelligent terminal programmed to handle word processing, but, as it turned out, I need not have worried because the first company I took the idea to practically bit my hand off and agreed to do the job for the ridiculously small fee of £750! The bonus was that I was shown around the Foreign Office and walked up the magnificent staircase installed, appropriately, at the height of the British Empire's ascendancy, presumably to impress visiting natives.

---

the appropriate petal to print each character as the carriage moved across the platen. It operated at up to 50 characters a second. It was invented by an engineer at Friden, but Friden refused to put it into production, even though it was then the obvious successor to typebars. Superseded some years later by inkjet printers.

Sales People

An indispensable part of business life – sales people – you either love 'em or loathe 'em, but they do make the world go around, and occasionally they come out with some great remarks. For example, at the afore-mentioned company, Arbat, which was majority owned by Arbuthnot Latham, which was then a small but old and prestigious merchant bank and member of the inner circle of accepting houses, there was a  meeting in Arbat's board room to show the company to Andy Arbuthnot, the tall, patrician, head of the bank. Geoff Harris, the small, moustachioed and rather portly managing director, was introduced to Mr Arbuthnot with the words, "Geoff is the leader of this band". To which one of my sales guys in earshot volunteered, "More like George Chisholm[2] than Sir Malcolm Sargent!"

Success in a sales career is really a matter of self-motivation, being prepared to keep on contacting people regardless of the turn-downs you receive. Most people give up far too easily, forgetting that there may be any number of reasons why their product or

---

2 Comedy jazz band leader of the 1960s

service is unwelcome at that particular moment. Those reasons usually have nothing to do with the quality of the offering or even the acceptability of the person offering it. Market intelligence can help to define the organisations likely to be interested, but things are rarely as simple as noting which organisations are on the up. For example, I, like many others, have found it particularly difficult to sell anything to travel agents or estate agents.

The reason for this appears to be that when things are good, they don't feel they need any aids to get more business – obviously, lunch is what is really required – and when things are bad, they can't afford anything – even lunch. The swing from one to the other seems to happen so quickly that I never actually arrived at an agency in the apparent nanosecond when their business was not in either state.

Of course, luck – and making the best of it – can play a significant part in making a sale. A case in point was my first interview at Friden in 1968 when I arrived, having been given an introduction by the Officers Association, which helped find jobs for retired military officers, and was unsure which of the two Mr Jacksons in the company was scheduled to see me. On asking, I was told that Paul Jackson was the Marketing Director and Ray Jackson the Regional Sales Manager. Naturally, I opted for the Director, who was, fortunately, available at that moment, and it was only later that I discovered that I was really meant to see Ray, who later told me he would never, with my then lack of sales experience, have given me a job in a month of Sundays.

Paul had been an officer in the Royal Navy and gave me a much gentler interview than Ray who was a tough, old-school sales manager. Paul asked me what I thought was the most important attribute of a salesman, and after some thought (and failing to find any better ideas), I replied, "Being nice to people". Long experience has since taught me that shit-hot salesmen without any scruples might succeed for a while, but in time, the word gets around, and sales become harder and harder. They then tended to sell whatever they could dream up and at any price and so got their company into serious trouble by promising more than it could provide.

A good example of the over-emphasis on sales above any other consideration is the meltdown in the banking business, where the desire to earn bonuses and lack of management control almost crashed the banking system and then the world's economic system. In spite of all the pontificating by authorities and experts, lessons are never learnt – or at least not for long – because three of the worst offenders, Lehman Bros., Goldman Sachs, and Citibank last time around, were, according to Professor Kenneth Galbraith, all major culprits in the crash of 1929. As George Bernard Shaw said, "If history repeats itself, and the unexpected always happens, how incapable must Man be of learning from experience."

When I was selling real-time banking and foreign exchange systems for Arbat, I was curious as to how every bank could be making a profit from the other banks in its Foreign Exchange business – if they were the winners, where were the losers? Nobody at Arbat seemed entirely sure of the reasons until I persisted and was told that it was a question of when the deals matured and that as long as the merry-go-round continued, everyone could make a profit, albeit some sooner than others. I then naively asked what would happen if it stopped, only to be told that that was impossible.

Well, Lehman Bros. going bust suddenly in September 2008 effectively stopped the banking merry-go-round, and everyone fell off. The aftermath of the mess the City has caused for the UK economy can best be described as Mammonia, the smell after the banks have pissed all over us – and then been compensated for their losses in doing so, as they were, and still are, perceived by politicians as too big to fail!

In fact, as a sales manager I found that it was possible, if you were prepared to put in some effort in training people, that even the most unlikely person could become reasonably successful in sales, provided they were prepared to stick at it. In the computer systems industry many of the most successful people had had a background in systems rather than sales and succeeded because they knew their onions, looked after their customers well and didn't oversell. Conversely good people from a sales background had usually taken the time and put in the effort to really understand the customer's problem and had developed good systems demonstrations to show off their solution.

In the early 1970s, when the Holy Grail of mainframe computing was seat reservation systems for airlines, I was faced with a similar problem for hospitals, which had a desperate need for a real-time bed allocation system. I knew that the costs of installing a mainframe computer in a hospital were out of all proportion to the likely benefits and felt that, if I could demonstrate a neat bed allocation system on a network of micro computers, this would have a major cost impact for hospitals by allowing them to allocate beds efficiently and capturing all the relevant patient data at the time of admission.

At that time, memory and processing power on these micros was extremely limited – something like 8K bytes of RAM storage, and they used magnetic tape cartridges on each machine and small 2.5 Mbyte discs on a central machine, so the trick was to come up with an algorithm rather than simply pigeon-holing the data to disc as one would with the comparatively massive memory available at very low-cost today.

After working on this problem for about six months and badgering every good systems person that I knew, one night, I suddenly woke up with the answer, rushed to the loo to write it down without disturbing my wife or children, tested it in the morning –

and it worked! It relied on the fact that only one person could be admitted at one moment in time at the one admission place in the hospital. So, using a neat trick, the programme modified itself and held the result in memory rather than accessing a memory store on tape or disc and updating it with new information – sounds crazy now, but it worked. A Regional Health Authority to whom I demonstrated it was convinced enough to buy the system for one of its hospitals, with the promise of a further ten hospitals once it was installed and running. Clearly, if successful, the system would have been adopted all over the country, as any other solution was at least five to ten times more expensive.

Unfortunately, before it could be delivered, Singer Business Machines was sold to ICL and, in spite of my telling the ICL people what we had done, they were not interested, as they were really only into mainframes at that time and clearly regarded networks of micros as some sort of fantasy. I left in disgust to join a systems company in the City (Arbat), and the hospital system I designed was, as far as I know, never installed. A pity because ICL, with its government leverage, could have ensured that almost every hospital in the UK bought the system at around £100,000 a throw, which would have saved ICL as a company and probably many thousands of lives lost through countless hospital administrative cock-ups since that time.

In fact, much of the patient record data capture and transmission required for the Health Service system, which they tried to install at a cost of over £12 billion during Tony Blair's Labour Government (though many informed experts say up to £30 billion), would have been unnecessary as the data would have been captured for many years already. Even the Labour government finally realised that this was another crap idea of Blair's (he knew absolutely nothing about computers and was sold on the idea by some consultants – as usual) and duly binned it, but only after spending £billions.

The take-over of Singer Business Machines was masterminded by Geoff "Tiger" Cross, the managing director of ICL, with the objective of broadening ICL's product line and reducing its dependence on the mainframe computer market where it was suffering from heavy competition with IBM, Burroughs, Univac, NCR, Honeywell and Control Data. Its sales at that point were, therefore, heavily dependent on support from the British Government, which gave it preference in all tenders unless ICL machines could not do the job. This led to all sorts of fudges and anomalies as departments tried to get around the restrictions or meekly accepted what ICL chose to provide.

Tiger Cross bought Singer BM for $30 million, which turned out to be an incredible bargain as the systems and machines sitting in stock at Singer were worth about $90 million. However, soon afterwards, he attracted much negative publicity because of some irregularities with his expenses, involving some dubious purchases to his personal benefit, and was forced to leave the company. This was a great pity as he was a great marketing man, and ICL's share of the market suffered considerably under the accountant who took over his job.

A year later, I spotted an article in the Business section of The Times which stated that the UK had three or four times more Chartered Accountants than any other country in Europe, so I wrote into their Letters column, under the heading *"This Monstrous Regiment of Accountants"*, identifying this as one of the reasons for the UK's then lack of international competitiveness and noting the experience of ICL where to avoid placing the company under the control of either the marketing or production people, the compromise figure was the accountant, who probably understood neither function.

The Times wanted me to drop the explicit reference to ICL – which, in order to get the letter published, I agreed to – and then deeply regretted as several of the letters in response wondered whether I had any particular company in mind. Obviously, other letters flooded into the paper from the heads of the various accountancy bodies and big accountancy firms, seeking to justify the relatively high numbers of accountants in the UK and the importance of their roles.

One of the most interesting aspects of being in computer system sales is the huge variety of systems that you get to see. For example, one of the very first computer systems I encountered in 1968 was a Leo III computer owned – proudly – by Lloyds Bank in what was then their computer centre in Poultry in the City of London. It had easily the most impressive set of indicator lights I have ever seen on a computer. There were about thirty of them mounted in a desk console, and they were the size of 100-watt electric bulbs and in various colours such as white, yellow, green and red. They flashed on and off as the programme went through its paces, lighting up the room like Piccadilly Circus.

However, the Ministry of Defence installations beat the lot, with the aircraft parts system at Hendon being by far the physically largest – if not the most powerful – that I have visited. Their ICL 1904 system was housed, along with fifty 10 Mbyte disc drives, each the size of a large washing machine, with wide aisles between them for cooling purposes, in a huge aircraft hangar. The total memory available was, therefore, less than a tenth of what you typically get in a mobile phone memory card nowadays, and the computer itself ran at less than a millionth of the speed of a smart mobile phone.

My days at Friden taught me that demonstrating systems successfully meant that you had to understand both the customer's problem that you were attempting to solve as well as, obviously, the capabilities of the system you were showing. If you were in command of your material, you could subtly steer the presentation so that the customer invariably asked the questions that you were well prepared to answer – rather, as a barrister in a court of law should never ask a witness a question that might provide a response detrimental to his case.

Of course, surprises do happen. One such being from a heavily-spectacled Japanese gentleman from a bank in the City who, when shown a system on two vast monitor screens, complained that he could not read them and, without warning, violently pushed forward the boardroom table that he was sitting behind in order to get a closer look. To demonstrate the system, I was, as normal, standing between that table and the desk on which were the screens, and so was pinned between his table and mine. To say the least, the demonstration did not get off to a good start, and I resolved to give Japanese banks a wider berth in future.

On another occasion, I had asked my boss, who was an expert at hard-wiring small machines, to set up the plug board of a simple add-punch – basically a programmable calculator with a paper tape punch – for me. The demonstration was quite simple and quick, and it seemed to work OK, so I duly gave the demonstration to an American bank, but noticed while answering their questions afterwards that smoke was coming out of the machine, so I hastily turned it off, which completely aborted the presentation. On questioning my boss about it later that day, he replied, "Oh, I knew that would happen. I hadn't set it up for real!" "Thanks a lot" was all I could manage to say. I never let him near another demonstration.

Demonstrating computer systems that were often in a prototype stage was always a chancy business, but the worst experience I ever suffered was when presenting Arbat's SWIFT banking payments system to a large audience from a number of banks. I had – perhaps unwisely – elected to use a voice input system to control the demonstration.

As anyone who has used an automatic banking system with voice input of responses in those days will vouch, it could be difficult to get a "hit" the first time. In the late 1970s, voice input systems were very fragile and one had to train the system to one's own voice, which I had previously done in a calm environment in our offices. However, in this presentation, there was naturally some stress in my voice, which got worse when the system refused to recognise me, so after some moments – which seemed like hours – we reverted to keyboard input, to everyone's evident relief.

Things do sometimes go without a hitch, even in 'mission critical' presentations, one such being to the Hong Kong Shanghai Bank in Hong Kong, when, after successfully demonstrating the SWIFT system, in a flush of enthusiasm, I mentioned that we also had a message switching system, whereupon, not surprisingly, the senior systems man at HSBC asked to see it. We had not prepared a demonstration, but the prototype system was on the disc we had brought with us, so I asked my colleague – a smashing guy called Mike Evans – who was operating the system for me, to send a message from one screen to the other. It worked like a dream, and we all departed to a luxurious private golf club to celebrate. Mike told me later that he had been shitting himself as it had never worked before, and indeed the entire system was subsequently re-written because they never managed to get the prototype version to send another message! The happy outcome was that the bank bought both systems for several locations in a £multi-million deal.

The Hong Kong trip, which fortunately only lasted two weeks, was a good example of what Thomas Watson, the founder of IBM, meant when he said, "Within us all, there are wells of thought and dynamos of energy which are not suspected until emergencies arise. Then oftentimes, we find that it is comparatively simple to double or triple our former capacities and to amaze ourselves by the results."

To prepare the presentation we had to use mini-computers at a computer service bureau which we found when we got there, was busy with other work during the day, so we could only work on them at night, with the result that we found ourselves working all night on the presentation and then all day contacting potential customers in Hong Kong. Even the Chinese thought this was over the top, and when we shrugged it off and pretended it was normal for us, they took us out to dinner at the Jumbo floating tourist restaurant at Aberdeen harbour and insisted that we eat the very tough steak they had ordered – with chopsticks!

I subsequently managed to sell SWIFT systems to some British banks in Hong Kong, and, on analysing the type of traffic they were sending and receiving, it was pretty clear that a good proportion of it was personal, as opposed to business, payments connected to the illegal drugs trade. Whether the bank was complicit in this is not for me to say, but it would have been comparatively simple for the authorities to monitor the traffic and arrest the parties involved if they had wished to do so.

Some years later, I sold a banking accounting system to a branch of an Irish bank located in New York and was told in confidence, after it had been installed, that the bank's primary objective in being in New York was to act as a conduit for funds from Irish-Americans to support terrorism in Northern Ireland and that the new system was expected to facilitate those payments.

Again, it is highly likely that the authorities knew exactly what was going on and turned a blind eye – this was long before 9/11. If these experiences are typical, and I am pretty sure they are, much of the world trade in illegal arms and drugs could be stopped, or at least made much more difficult, by having the authorities clamp down hard on the money channels, i.e. banks, through which the payments are made. The absurd money laundering regulations that impede so many large and small one-off personal transactions are completely irrelevant to stopping such business.

Ultra-respectable banks can also be more obviously complicit in protection rackets, as a great friend, Jos Roberts, who was a very talented industrial designer, found in New York whilst doing design work on the Forex dealing room of a major Swiss bank. One morning he was told by his liaison man at the bank that there was someone waiting to see him. He was shown into a small room where his contact advised him to co-operate and then left him with a very shady-looking character in black shades and a sharp suit who asked him what work he was doing for the bank and how much he was charging for it. Jos attempted to skirt round the question until the guy said, "Look, I don't think you limeys understand the situation – nothing gets done around here without our say-so". Jos suddenly realised that he was meeting the mafia in person – condoned by the bank – so he had no choice but to co-operate.

In the late 1970s, I sold a message-switching system to BCCI – yes, the notorious Bank for Credit and Commerce International that went bust some years later. I must say that it always gave me a very uncomfortable feeling when visiting the bank. I guess it was the combination of opulence and bad taste, which, in my experience, often means that something is wrong, plus the fact that one very rarely saw anyone waiting in the reception area, which indicated a lack of business coming through wholesale banking channels.

However, needs must, and we installed the system and got it working.

But there was a weak point in the system because, to preserve its income stream, BT insisted that some of its own-manufactured modems were installed between the system and its telex lines. These modems had a defective design, which meant that they were capable, off their own bat, of sending an answerback or acknowledgement, even if the incoming message had not yet been safely stored for some reason. Unfortunately, such a message was sent from Pakistan telling the bank that its founder, Hassan Abedi, would be arriving at Heathrow at such-and-such a date and time. The result was that he was not met there and was so angry that he ordered that our system be thrown out; so we just agreed to remove it, as we could install the hardware elsewhere.

Sometime later, I recounted this story to a fairly senior figure in the City who asked if we had been paid for the system and when I admitted that we hadn't, he replied that he would have been very surprised if we had ever been paid, whether the system worked or not! So, it was well known in the City that BCCI were a dodgy outfit many years before its dealings in drugs and arms were exposed and – even worse – before it took over a respectable American bank by "stealth", which finally forced the authorities there to act and close it down.

There was an interesting postscript in that I asked the IT manager at BCCI, who was an ex-IBM salesman if we could demonstrate the system to Thomas Cook, the travel agent before the bank had it removed. He agreed and proceeded to give the most magnificent presentation to the travel people, extolling the system's virtues and producing benefits that I would never have thought of! Obviously Thos. Cook bought the system – they could hardly do otherwise. Clearly, he had been a top salesman and perhaps even felt guilty about the way things had turned out, as he well knew we were the innocent party.

In 1982 one of my sales team told me he had visited BCCI and that they were a good prospect for a banking system. I told him that if he visited them again or even talked to them, I would regard it as a sackable offence – this was some eight years before the bank went bust. I discussed BCCI with several bankers and asked them why it was allowed to carry on for so long when everyone knew it was a scam. They replied that the other banks benefited because BCCI had to pay more for overnight deposits than any other bank in the City because of its bad reputation and that this was good business for them because BCCI was unlikely to go bust overnight! Nobody gave a damn about the innocent 36,000 depositors in the UK who lost almost all their money – least of all the regulator, the Bank of England, whose bank oversight department was headed at that time by 'Steady' Eddie George. In fact, he and the Bank shuffled the responsibility off to Luxembourg – that well-known centre of bank openness and probity – where BCCI, for tax reasons, had its nominal HQ.

At Arbat in the late 1970s, I was invited by the Bank of England to propose a Voice Input system to handle the identification of the individual gold bars that arrived in those days every fortnight from the mines in South Africa by ship to Southampton and then by lorry to the Bank. On arrival in their vaults, the bars were individually weighed and identified by number.

It was decided to input this data into a system and I proposed a similar system that we had installed in De Beers for weighing and identifying pouches of diamonds, with the weighing machine being linked digitally to an input port on the computer. The Voice Input system would allow the gold bar handler to speak in the specific number stamped into each bar as it was weighed, which would be much quicker and more accurate than using a keyboard to input both details.

Inevitably, the Bank thought our system was too expensive and installed a simple keyboard and screen linked to their mainframe. The problem was that all keyboards at that time used a system of gold-plated connections and, alas, there was so much gold dust in the atmosphere in the vaults that they never got their system to work – whereas our voice input system just used a microphone and display in the main bullion room. My only consolation was that I am one of the few people to be able to accuse the Bank of England – with justification – of being too cheap to do their job properly!

In the 1970s, I sold a SWIFT interface system to Hambros Bank in Brentwood and suggested they opt for a new type of Digital Equipment PDP system, which had a single long cabinet on wheels, including the processor and twin disc drives. This proved to be too big to get into their lift, so they decided to use a 'stair-walker', which was a platform that cleverly climbed the stairs with the computer cabinet sitting on it. Naturally, it was an electrically powered machine plugged into the mains, and yes, you guessed it, the cable was not long enough. The stair-walker unplugged itself, and the whole lot crashed back downstairs to the ground floor, wrecking the computer. Fortunately, no one was hurt, and even more fortunately, we were able to book a second order to replace the first machine. Bill Davis, who at that time ran their systems, took it in good part, as it wasn't actually our fault, and even went on to order a second (third?) system for message switching. He – deservedly – later went on to run the bank.

After I left Arbat, I had lunch with Bill and obviously told him the saga of what had happened at Arbat over the electronic mail system and that I considered they had behaved very stupidly. It is interesting to note that Arbat never really sold any more systems to banks, though whether that was down to Bill spreading the word amongst his extensive contacts in the City, I would not know – and never asked.

One of the best pieces of advice on selling was given to me on my initial sales training course when Paul Jackson told us about a friend of his who worked for one of the major aircraft manufacturers in the US and was trying to close a huge deal for 20 or so aircraft to an airline. Apparently, he gave the presentation and made his pitch and then – SHUT UP! He knew that if he opened his mouth, he would lose the sale, so everyone sat there in silence for 20 minutes until, finally, one of the people from the airline cracked up and said something. Paul Jackson's friend got his sale. The thinking behind this is that it is very easy to talk yourself out of a sale by blithering on after making your pitch. You can open up all sorts of possibilities for the customer to procrastinate over, whereas if you keep silent, the pressure is on him (or her).

Offices and their Meanings

Another aspect of the salesman's life is visiting an enormous number of offices and observing what effect they have, both on the visitor and on the incumbents. I have already mentioned the odd atmosphere in the office at BCCI and that it was an interesting example of extremely bad taste allied with excessive expenditure. The whole place was decorated in a nasty shade of what can only be described as shit brown, and this was maintained throughout the upper floors with an open plan effect so that as you walked through to meet your contact, you could see the down-trodden wage slaves cowering at their desks. Naturally, this created a very bad impression on a visitor – quite the opposite of what was intended.

Other notable offices I visited included Barings Bank, where I met the elderly white-haired "computer manager" who, some years before the Nick Leeson disaster, presided over an antiquated magnetic stripe ledger card system from NCR, which would have had its hands full providing adequate management control information on any sort of regular basis – certainly not in real-time. Indeed, the computer room was a beautiful mahogany-lined office dating from the 19th century. The striking thing was that the manager saw no need for anything more up-to-date. A disaster waiting to happen? Not surprisingly, the need to get up to speed and compete with other banks led directly to the bank's demise by allowing a trader in the Far East control over his own back office operations. Their computer systems should have prevented this and indeed informed the management that unacceptable actions were going on long before the train hit the buffers.

The offices of senior management can be quite creepy, for example, that of the head of Citibank in Bush House at Aldwych in the 1970s, which featured a small conference room off his office with a glass wall which was a one-way mirror so that he could see into it from his desk, but the occupants of the conference room could not see out. To enter his office, you went down three stairs immediately inside the door, which was fine, but on your way out, you had to simultaneously climb the stairs and open the door. I believe that the purpose of this layout was to discomfit the visitor when the supremo asked a question as someone left the room, resulting in a stumble backwards by the unfortunate down into the manager's office. Louis B. Mayer's office in Hollywood featured a similar device.

In fact, the reason I and Doug Schilling went there was because we were proposing to Citibank, who was already a customer for our communications systems, that they purchase a geo-stationary satellite over the Atlantic to handle all their American-European communications and be able to sell-off any spare capacity to third parties. Quite a novel concept in the late 1970s.

The CEO obviously thought it was a good idea, as we were allowed to leave without any last-second questions. I found out later that they went ahead with the satellite when I met a consultant  who, to my annoyance, had actually implemented our project. More about consultants later. Citibank had previously bought a SWIFT interface system from me, and my contact there, Martin Wake, who ran their systems operation, became rather a friend. I asked him whether he found it a problem working at such a hard-nosed – to put it politely – organisation such as Citibank. He replied that he had previously worked for Emil Savundra at Fire, Auto and Marine Insurance and Bernie Cornfeld at IOS (the two major financial scams of the 1960s and 1970s), so Citibank was a breeze!

Offices can also be scarily dangerous, which I discovered after selling a system to Lloyds Bank, who at that time had an office in Cannon Street, which had been built in the early 1970s by John Poulson, the infamous 'architect' and developer from Tyneside, finally found guilty of bribery and corruption and jailed some years later.

Apparently, the upper floors were so weak that filing cabinets could only be positioned near the walls and in order to install the minicomputer we sold them it had to be placed on a metal plate to spread the load. The people there told me they never ate in the staff canteen on the top floor because the cracks in the walls were large enough to put your fist into. At around that time, Lloyds built a huge computer centre on the south side of the river near Blackfriars Bridge, which was supposed to be impervious to nuclear attack unless it suffered a direct hit. Whether it would have had any customers to serve after such a strike on London seems not to have occurred to the people who commissioned such an expensive, purpose-built building.

Further along the South Bank, the building that is now Tate Modern was previously owned and inhabited by the Central Electricity Generating Board, which had its main computing centre in an annexe on the south side of the power station. This featured some huge zinc extractor vents on its flat roof, and on one occasion, when I visited the site, they had all disappeared. I mentioned this to my contact there and said how much better the building looked without them, and he replied that several of them had just fallen off and that the computer system had had to be shut down as the cooling system no longer worked.

I asked why they had fallen off, only to be told that the fumes from the coal-powered power station next door had corroded them through. What the fumes were doing to the local populace is not recorded. In fact, the system I was trying to sell the CEGB was to be installed at a customer of theirs that monitored and collected data on landslips in Wales, data which was then transmitted to and processed at the said computer centre. Unfortunately the order fell through when the monitoring station was itself buried by – you guessed it – a landslip.

The Lloyds of London insurance market building in the City was, and still is, hugely controversial, with its innards on display on the outside in order to allow large open spaces on the inside. Milord Rogers gained many accolades and awards for this, all of which ignored the fact that the reason water and other services are normally buried within a building is to minimise corrosion from the elements, something that is becoming more apparent as the building ages.

Lord Rogers also failed to allow for computer cables linking terminals to the systems to be accommodated, providing only a small diameter hole of about 12 inches at the corner of each floor. The result is that false floors have had to be installed, ruining the appearance and convenience of much of the interior. Lloyds' other problem is that the entrance is below ground level and very much less than impressive when eventually you do find it. In fact, a much more graceful and beautiful building had been erected in Cannon Street a few years earlier, with its services and structure carried in an external lattice work of stainless steel pipes arranged like a trellis and contrasting beautifully with the dark glass walls. Neat, effective and homogenous, why could Rogers not do likewise?

The other problem with mega-buildings is that so much corporate time and energy is focused on them that the business often suffers, not to mention the megalomaniac mindset that then seems to possess the occupants. It can be no coincidence that the Lloyds scandals, when new recently-recruited members were deliberately put into syndicates that were then stuffed with bad, often asbestosis, risks, occurred at the same time that the move was being made to the new building. I have often noted this syndrome.

For example, I visited the Arthur Andersen Consulting building near Charing Cross a few months before Andersen went spectacularly bust and was confronted in their reception area with marble floors, pillars and walls and, unbelievably, a large marble fountain. What was a firm of accountants and consultants doing trying to emulate Ancient Rome? I even found the same thing at Nixdorf Computer's new building in Bracknell, which also featured marble halls and a huge fountain, all in the worst possible taste. The 9-acre site had cost £14 million, plus many more millions spent on the building itself.

Why did a relatively small German computer firm – at least in this country – need such a huge building on such a vast site? Inevitably, Nixdorf went bust a couple of years later. Mike Hart was in charge of the UK operation at the time and boasted that it was his greatest achievement. Any sensible customer wonders if his bill would have been less if his supplier had been less extravagant. I once had a job interview at Univac, which inhabited twin towers on the North Circular Road, and whilst waiting in their reception area, noted that the floor carpet extended in a curve up the walls, giving the feeling of a sanatorium for the self-harming. The impression of a madhouse was confirmed when I noted that several huge black limos were waiting in open garages outside with their engines running and uniformed chauffeurs standing by – ready for a fast getaway?

In contrast, when I first joined Virgin in the late 1980s, Richard Branson's office was in a canal boat in Little Venice. Apparently, the decking leaked atrociously in rainy weather and the interior was

part office, part living accommodation for Richard. The result was that no one in the organisation could make a fuss about the standard of their office, and in fact, when a substantial new building was acquired for Virgin Retail, Branson then

"I'll let you know when a better office becomes available..."

received a good offer of about £4 million for it and promptly sold it at a handsome profit before Retail had moved in!

Naturally they were not too happy about it as their old accommodation was terribly cramped, to which he apparently replied that the property deal had made far more money than Retail would, in that year, at any rate. At least they had a staircase in their office; our Virgin Games' office in Vernon's Yard, off the Portobello Road, had only a ladder to get upstairs, to begin with!

While at Virgin I learnt that any publishing operation needs to keep its overheads as low as possible because the cyclical nature of publishing means that even if one year is good, there is no probability that the next one will be. This is why it was a financial disaster for Harper Collins when they moved all their various small publishing outfits into huge new offices near Hammersmith, because suddenly each outfit had to cover their share of the vastly increased office costs without any concomitant increase in revenue, let alone profits.

The huge atrium in the centre of the building, which went from floor to roof, was surrounded by metal stairways and, walkways and railings, which gave the complete heebie-jeebies to many of the staff who suffered from vertigo. The expensive trees that were placed in the middle of the atrium grew so quickly in the favourable atmosphere that they soon had to be replaced. I was told when I was trying desperately to finalise a licensing contract with Harpers for

Halliwell's Film Guide that their lawyer when he finally returned from holiday, was going to be busy for more than a week re-organising his filing system and cabinets! Needless to say, the deadline passed, and the agreement fell by the wayside. You have to ask yourself which was more important – a neat filing system or a deal potentially worth many thousands of pounds to all concerned?

The Royal Bank of Scotland "World Headquarters" at Gogarburn, built at the behest of Sir Fred Godwin in the lead-up to the bank going spectacularly bust in 2008, has enough fountains – outside the building this time, set in a small lake, together with trees inside in its "internal street", to satisfy the most aesthetic architect. Indeed, the architect's own description beggars belief – reading it, it is hard to recall that RBS is/was just a bank, for heavens' sake!

"The design provides a 'world-class' facility for RBSG. Set in its own landscaped campus-style grounds, it consists of a world headquarters building comprising six office pavilions and an executive pavilion with an entrance hall focused on an internal street; together

56

with ancillary accommodation and the potential for two further office developments. The internal street, enclosed by an elegant steel and glass structure, provides facilities such as a retail bank, convenience food outlets, a grocery store and restaurants. The ancillary facilities include a conference and training centre, nursery, leisure centre and staff club with additional services such as doctor, dentist and hairdresser. The landscape incorporates the hydrology and surface water attenuation without affecting, possibly even enhancing, its visual impact."

On a smaller scale, the Dunfermline Building Society housed 500 of its headquarters' employees in a huge glass structure out of all proportion to its revenues and importance – and went bust soon after. Its sense of its own importance was typified by, for example, the naming of its "Destiny" software project. There are numerous such examples in every business sector, and the truth is that shareholders should get really nervous when they hear a pompous announcement that the business **they** own is moving itself to a purpose-built new headquarters – and if it includes any of the words "architect-designed, glass structure, fountains and marble" – head for the exit, fast!

I have no prejudice against great architecture; in fact, I love it, but I do question whether it should be paid for by the shareholders of a business, who will have had no hand in the decision to proceed with it, particularly as its most apparent benefit is to enable the management of the business to show off to their friends or business acquaintances.

What contribution, after all, does a swanky head office make to a bank's bottom line? A bank is not like a factory that requires specially built facilities to utilise new technology in order to reduce costs; all you need is somewhere to put people with telephone lines, desks and computers. In fact, in the case of RBS, it was even worse because the bank had vacated its beautiful Palladian headquarters in the New Town in the centre of Edinburgh, where at least the customers could easily see and admire the building – which they had not paid to build – and feel satisfied that their bank was solid. None of the customers would ordinarily see Gogarburn, built at a cost of £335 million!

Still, I suppose that Scottish business has come a long way from my first visit to the National Savings Bank in Cowglen near Glasgow in the early 1970s when, in a taxi in one of the less salubrious streets, we encountered a French onion seller in beret on his traditional bicycle with a large sack of onions tied to the front handlebars, toiling up the hill. Nearing the top, the bag burst and onions began rolling down the street, bouncing on the pavements and ricocheting off walls. Instantly the almost empty street was filled with old biddies in black coats who appeared from nowhere and snaffled all the onions, stuffing them into bags, stuffing them up their skirts and down their fronts. It was all over in a few seconds, and the old biddies disappeared, leaving the poor onion seller alone with his bike, and this time his tears were from an absence of onions and not from their fumes.

In due course, I arrived at Cowglen and was ushered into their canteen for a quick lunch. The chat going on at the tables around us was easily audible, and at first, I thought they were putting on imitation Billy Connolly-type accents for my benefit until I eventually realised they must be for real. The machine room at Cowglen had about 25 automatic typewriters that I had sold them to print new savings books, invariably manned by ladies, who, after several visits, I got to know quite well, and as they discovered I had been in the Army, I used to play up to it by entering their vast machine room and saying in a loud military voice "Stand by your beds!", which went down quite well. However, on a later occasion, when I had not visited them for some time, I came in and gave the command as usual to be greeted with a stunned silence; they had recruited an entirely new set of girls.

Perhaps the most beautiful bank building I ever visited is the headquarters of the Bank for International Settlements in Basle. It is an amazing circular building, wider at the base and at the top, like an hourglass, though not as accentuated, with spectacular views of the Alps from all its main offices. In fact, the views are so wonderful that it must be hard for the occupants to actually concentrate on their work; perhaps this is one of the reasons that the bank has attracted so much criticism over the years.

The ultimate office buildings of their time, the unfortunate World Trade Centre towers in New York, always had a rather cheap, tacky feel about them, both inside and out, and were undoubtedly very undistinguished architecturally, being just very tall square blocks. Sadly, this cheapness proved to be their undoing as it is now clear that had they been built to satisfactory standards, practically – as well as aesthetically – like the Empire State (which also had a plane fly into it) or Rockefeller Centre, probably many, if not all, of the victims of the attack who were trapped on the upper floors, could have escaped down the central stairways. Ignoring building regulations, or at least not using best practices, makes all the difference.

Health & Safety inspectors in the UK seem to have an agenda all of their own. I remember being deputed by my boss to take an inspector round Singer Business Machines' then fairly modern office building on Blackfriars Road, and the only thing the inspector was interested in was whether it was a union shop or not. How that impacted H&S is a complete mystery to me, and as there was quite a lot of electrical and mechanical equipment in the offices and workshops, there were actually plenty of things to inspect. If there had been proper, regular H&S inspections of more difficult environments in the North Sea, especially the Piper Alpha platform, would that disaster have happened?

Managers – The Good, the Bad and the Ugly

The best manager that I ever worked for was a true, old-school sales professional called Tom Bearley, who had been in the business for many years and, in fact, had run the sales training programme for Friden, which was brilliantly constructed and well ahead of its time for the late 1960s. For example, he instituted the use of videotape machines to film, and subsequently playback, "customer meetings" that had been set up in-house between various experienced managers in Singer and the trainees. At that time, the only video tape recording machines available were huge, studio-quality, Ampex machines and large cameras, so the experience was a totally new one for all the tyro salesmen.

Unbelievably, the course lasted for six weeks, something that is virtually unknown nowadays because almost no company would invest that sort of time in sales training. Tom persuaded the company's top salesmen to come in from the field and discuss their sales approach and their successes in an effort to enthuse and inspire the trainees.

The actual sales training was subcontracted to the Tack organisation, which is still ongoing, and a remarkable guy called Eddy Hutchinson ran the course. He had the habit of standing in front of us with one foot on the top of a desk and his knee consequently bent up into his chest, as he was not a very tall man. It looked most peculiar and could not have been all that comfortable, but nonetheless, he was a very good trainer with a great sense of humour.

Tom, I am certain, was sorely tried by some of my rather off-the-wall sales tactics, particularly when I presented him with sales *faits accompli* when I knew that he would have little choice but to accept the order, even though it was bound to present some problems in delivery. My view was that I probably knew better than him whether the system would actually work – and fortunately, I was usually right – so giving him the opportunity to kibosh it before we had confirmed the order would not be in either of our interests.

I got some dreadful bollockings en route, but Tom generally went along with my system, and a year or two after I left Singer, walking along near Aldwych with my next boss, we by chance met Tom in Fleet Street, and Tom was kind enough to say to him "William is a sticker", meaning that I didn't ever give up. That story always reminds me of the graffiti on the Hammersmith flyover next to the usual official "Bill Stickers will be prosecuted" – "Bill Sticker is innocent!". Other favourite graffiti there were "Jesus Saves – St. John[3] scores from the other end" and "Fart for Peace".

My first boss, Robbie Roberts, the manager of the City Branch, was a nightmare and totally unsuited to be a manager of anything, although he did have a good knowledge of the old paper-tape

---

3 Ian St. John was a prodigious Liverpool FC and Scotland striker in the 1960s

systems machines that Friden had made for many years, and consequently had been a successful salesman in his day. He smoked so incessantly that his office was always filled with smoke, and one went into it for a sales meeting at one's peril. Generally, all you could see through the glass wall partitions of his office was a cloud of blue smoke and faint, ghostly figures appearing dimly through the haze. Robbie, though a kindly man, was clearly not adapting to the whirlwind of change brought about by the advent of electronics, as opposed to the electro-mechanics that he was used to, and left the firm in a shake-up that coincided with the 1974 recession.

Less wholesome was another character, also called Roberts (but no relation), who managed the London West branch and who realised that there was a good and highly profitable market, in selling second-hand machines. He, therefore, demanded sales forecasts from his team as usual and then contacted the companies concerned and flogged them good second-hand machines on the cheap that he had heard were coming off maintenance contracts from older installations. Rather than the manager's commission of about 1-2% on a £1,500 new machine, he was clearing £600-700 on an old machine doing the same job. Of course, his sales guys complained that they were losing sales, and though he cut some of them in on the deals, eventually, it all came out, and everyone concerned was fired.

A not-dissimilar scam was worked by the logistics manager at Nixdorf Computer in Germany who was in charge of PC procurement. Apparently, he made millions by having the company buy in portable/luggable PCs from Panasonic and then had a lorry arrive after work, loaded them all up at the back exit and later sold them on to Nixdorf again through the front door! He was in charge of the stores so he fixed the stock reports, and all was hunky-dory until suspicions were raised in top management when PCs were not available for demonstration, though the stock sheets showed thousands of them. He had bought a Schloss in what was then East Germany, on the profits, and was driving a top-of-the-range Mercedes, so it was surprising that no one noticed. He and some associates in on the deal wound up in jail.

Needless to say, good sales managers are hard to find, and often, good salesmen do not make good managers, usually because they find it easier to do everything themselves – that way, they know it is done right – with the result that the guys working for them if they are any good, get frustrated and leave. I found it was hard to maintain the right level of involvement so that we got an important sale, whilst allowing my sales people enough freedom to learn by making their own mistakes. I never went quite as far as the head of IBM, who said, "You can be discouraged by failure, or you can learn from it. So go ahead and make mistakes, make all you can. Because, remember, that's where you'll find success – on the far side of failure." Perhaps I should have.

A case in point was a sale Nixdorf made to the Post Office for hundreds of on-counter terminals. I had a great guy called Tony Makolski working for me whose account the Post Office was, and he was essentially a good systems man, turned salesman, though Nixdorf had not invested anything in re-training him. I knew this project was coming up, so I enlisted the aid of an old friend of my parents-in-law, who was a very influential financial figure in Mrs Thatcher's government.

He discreetly opened some doors for us, and we wound up taking a number of influential Post Office people out to Brussels for the annual conference event (and party) that Nixdorf ran for their banking customers. After a hard day's 'conferring', there was a Gala Evening to which everyone was invited; however, the Post Office people begged off (to Nixdorf's management's surprise) and asked me to take them out to dinner... etc. Well, the etc., turned out to be a nightclub (which I had been to before), and we were all sitting around a large table in a booth watching the strip show. I had warned the Post Office people on the way there that on no account were any of us to offer any of the girls a drink or even a cigarette so that there would be no feeling on the girls' part that we were trying to purchase their "services".

In the event, the top girl in the show was a Lancastrian who, in due course, gravitated to our table, where, needless to say, we refused her blandishments to buy her, and several of her colleagues who also turned up any kind of drink. Being from Yorkshire, I maintained that, obviously, Yorkshire gals were superior in every way, including bed, to Lancashire girls. This banter went on, with much hilarity, including several invitations from us to show us exactly how and why Lancastrian girls were better, and many interjections from the PO people for several hours, and we never did buy her a drink, to the visible fury of the club's management.

The PO people said this was the best night out they had ever had, and we got a large order soon afterwards. Tony Makolski had been away and not able to be included in the Brussels trip and I never did have the heart to tell him the real reasons he had got the order. As a sales manager, I worked to Robert Townsend's precept that "A leader is not an administrator who loves to run others, but someone who carries water for his people so that they can get on with their jobs". Interestingly, Richard Feynman, the world-famous physicist and a habitué of dubious bars after the premature death of his beloved wife, advocated exactly the same approach to the ladies he found in them in his autobiography, *"Surely you're joking, Mr Feynman?"*

This PO system was installed many years before the Fujitsu "Horizon" system, which turned into probably the biggest scandal of this century when the Post Office chose to blame their sub-postmasters for inaccuracies in their weekly accounts, demand repayment of huge sums of money running into £tens of thousands per Post Office, take them to court and happily see them imprisoned, all the while knowing quite well that their Horizon computer system had caused these problems. Bravely, a group of sub-postmasters stood up to the giant Post Office organisation, though they were not even supported by their union (which was subsidised to the tune of £ 1 million a year by the Post Office).

However, earlier last year, they won in court, though they were forced to accept a poor settlement, decimated by their legal costs, which had deliberately been run up by the Post Office in the, as it turned out, vain hope that they would be forced to abandon the case.

This is a prime example of a big organisation, the Post Office which was a body owned ultimately by the Government, behaving atrociously to small businesses dependent on it. Inevitably, none of the miscreants, read "criminals", at the Post Office, nor Fujitsu, have been sanctioned in any way. Indeed, the then head of the Post Office, Paula Vennells, was given a CBE and was appointed head of the Imperial College Healthcare NHS Trust. Incidentally, the word miscreant originally referred to the stocks where miscreants were pelted with rotten garbage, which it would, at least in this case, be opportune to re-instate.

Using my approach to 'entertaining the troops' can work in reverse, of course, and on a subsequent trip abroad with Tony Makolski and some gentlemen from a Scottish bank, we found ourselves in a large cavernous bar in Copenhagen (where we were going to visit a bank installation next day), sitting at long tables. After a while, two ladies appeared in fishnet tights, high heels, satin basques and frilly knickers. Naturally, I assumed that they were the place's "entertainment" and following my normal practice, refused point blank to buy them a drink, much to their surprise and to the astonishment of the surrounding Scotsmen. The girls even asked what my problem was, which was not an easy one to answer, and they soon went off with one of our party to a nearby jazz bar.

I discovered later that there was some sort of annual festival going on in Copenhagen and that people, especially women, adopted fancy dress and went out on the toot. Unfortunately, this incident set a negative tone for the whole trip, as the Scotsmen (for heaven's sake) thought I was being unduly mean and a real party pooper. We did not get the subsequent order – though there were systems and support problems making life difficult for us as well.

The management at Virgin had a different approach to any other I have encountered, and the guy who hired me, Nick Alexander, known in the industry as the "Laughing Shark", was a great manager and succeeded in making every meeting instructive, interesting and fun – a big contrast to the computer industry. He ran a very tight ship with no unnecessary expenditure and made it clear that if you wanted budget approval for something, you had to go out and find funds from companies who thought they would benefit from an association with the Virgin name, and he would then get the deal approved internally.

Unfortunately, his boss, Robert Devereux, was much less decisive – though in every other way the nicest and most charming guy you could meet – and I believe that Nick did his best to keep Robert out of our offices; certainly, I only ever saw him there on one occasion in a period of four years. Robert, though very receptive to my idea of a large-scale digital mapping project on CD-ROM – this was before the Internet took off – simply could not make up his mind about it, so when it was finally delivered – with an MTV-type front-end! – it was several years late and too watered down to appeal to its original markets in education and for reference works.

In the process, I had suggested, but he had rejected, three different ways of financing it with various partners before he decided Virgin should go it alone, though I did not benefit, as by then I had left Virgin and was working for them as a consultant. While this was dragging on, one of the partners that I had proposed should help us with the financing of the project took up the idea themselves, did it properly with their own CD-ROM product and wound up selling 3 million copies. This was the predecessor to Google Earth and Google Maps.

A year or two after this, Nick left Virgin and went to head up the games console people, Sega, in the UK, but before he left, he warned me about his successor, Tony Cheetham. I had negotiated a contract with a friend in the Far East to allow his company, Asia-CD, to manufacture and distribute several Virgin Games' products on CD-ROM exclusively in that part of the world. The contract promised me a commission of about 10%, which Cheetham refused to pay me after Virgin let an identical contract for the same products to another company in the same geographical area, and so, not surprisingly, Asia-CD cancelled their contract.

My lawyer issued a Statutory Declaration on Virgin which gave them 30 days to pay up in full, or the entire Virgin Group would be put, automatically, into liquidation when that period expired. As it happened, the thirty days were up on a Friday, and I waited in the office all day until, at about 4.50 pm, a motorcyclist courier appeared with a cheque. The cheque was for about £17,500, but I wondered what it would have been worth to me if the courier had not appeared and the thirty days had passed – £millions? Virgin at that time was valued at about £1 billion. Anyway I felt that I would be doing Richard Branson a favour if I wrote to him to tell him just what a prat he was employing. I believe Mr. Cheetham – an appropriate name – was invited to find other employment soon afterwards.

During my time at Virgin, I was asked to help get rid of a small company which Virgin had bought into a couple of years earlier that provided music over the telephone, using voice output technology to interact with the user who used the telephone keypad to request the latest pop record hits. It had cost Virgin just over half a million pounds, and despite its annual loss, they, in the form of Don Cruickshank, were expecting to sell it for approximately the same amount they had bought it for.

Don Cruickshank, later Sir Donald, was then working for Virgin and was responsible for sorting out this particular mess. He was subsequently appointed head of Oftel, was made Chairman of the London Stock Exchange and was appointed by Gordon Brown to review the UK banking sector in 1998 and from 1997 to 2000; he also served as Chairman of Action 2000, the U.K.'s Millennium Bug campaign. I spent quite a lot of time with the management of the telephone music company and realised that they wanted to do a management buyout backed by a venture capital fund. I pointed out to Don that they were prepared to offer £150,000 and that the only other offer was for about £50,000. I also told him that the only way to get more money out of the company was to enter the porn market, which would cause problems for Virgin and might result in the termination of their licence from BT.

Don was not happy about the situation, blamed me and took me off the deal – but wound up selling the company for £150k anyway. Actually, the company was not worth even that, as it went bust soon afterwards. Perhaps not Sir Donald's finest hour, though the Millennium Bug and the banking sector review hardly seem like great successes in hindsight.

Virgin was, at that time, regarded with some disfavour by the City because Branson had, a year or two previously, taken the company public in order to raise funds, but he found that the City's estimation of the value of the company was significantly at odds with what he regarded as its true worth, and was annoyed that the share price had drifted downwards from its offer price of about 120p, to around 90p. Branson knew that the value of the company had actually increased significantly during the same period, so he determined to buy the shares back – at the original offer price!

This was completely unprecedented and an amazingly honest and genuine thing to do because, as a result, none of the Virgin shareholders, some of them his friends, would lose a penny. Nonetheless, the City regarded it with great suspicion, and the only explanation can be that he had inadvertently exposed the share hyping, racketeering and inside dealing, which was (and I believe still is) common practice in the City. These City practices were designed to either overvalue shares so that those in the know already owning the company's shares could make a killing and then sell out before their dupes realised it, or in Virgin's case, undervalue the shares so that they would be an easy – and cheap – target for a takeover.

Interestingly, a few months after Branson had bought back the shares, he managed to sell half the record company to Fuji for about £450 million, or rather more than the City's valuation of the entire group, which also included the airline, broadcast facilities and a number of other businesses. This sale was apparently something of a relief as he had had to borrow extensively to buy back the shares and was paying the banks about £5 million a year in interest.

The only parallel instance that I can think of was the legacy by Heinz Nixdorf. After he died unexpectedly in 1986 at the Hanover Fair, or CeBit, a huge annual computer fair at which Nixdorf Computer had a major presence, his will set up what was then the world's largest computer museum in his home town of Paderborn (closed due to Covid-19 and never re-opened), and what's more, he left approximately £3,000 to each of his employees that had served five years or more with the company.

His achievement had been considerable. He founded the business in 1952 and built it up by 1986 to be the world's fourth-largest computer company, with over 25,000 employees. I only met him once, which was on the tarmac at Paderborn airport when I was waiting to hitch a lift on the company Learjet, along with several senior executives who were travelling to attend a Press conference in London. He was proudly singing the praises of his new company jet and comparing it favourably with a larger HS125 that was also sitting on the tarmac nearby.

I mentioned quietly afterwards to the Learjet pilots that I did not feel that he was comparing like with like as the HS125 was really a small airliner, as opposed to the Learjet, which looked like a flying cigar tube and that the HS125 was a direct successor to the Airspeed planes that my father had created with Nevile Shute in the 1930s. A rather sad postscript to this was the disappearance over the Atlantic a year or two later of Nixdorf's newly purchased twin-jet Cessna Citation, which was on its delivery flight from the factory in America to Paderborn. Neither pilot was ever found.

To divert for a moment, a marvellous guy, Derek Morley, who I brought into my team at Nixdorf, had been at Singer as part of a high-profile sales operation selling their Factory Data Collection System. He told me that he was part of the sales team accompanying the people from Hawker Siddeley, flying in one of their HS125s to see a similar Singer system installed at BAe, Filton. The senior guy from HS said "But why should we buy **your** FDC System when we make our own (which indeed they did)?" Derek replied, "Would you fly in an aircraft that Singer had made?" Game over – and sale made!

In spite of these rather high-profile modes of transport, Heinz Nixdorf drove around in an old NSU RO80 Wankel-engined saloon car and incidentally lived in a relatively modest house that he had owned for many years in Paderborn. His real power in the company, apart from his shareholding, was that no significant computer line was produced without his say-so. Apparently, owners of RO80s in the UK, when they passed another RO80 owner, used to hold up a hand with several fingers extended to indicate how many times the engine in their car had had to be replaced. In order to stay in the market, NSU had to replace the Wankel engines free of charge whenever they blew, which was pretty frequently! As Arno Bohn found at Porsche, computer people were not often experts on cars, nor indeed aeroplanes.

I had a terrifying experience taking a group of people from a Midlands-based Building Society to Paderborn. At my manager, Mike Hart's, behest, we had contracted with a neighbour/friend of his, who had just left British Airways to start his own charter business, to fly about eight of us in a twin-engined turbo-prop from Birmingham to Paderborn to show them the Nixdorf factory and a German savings bank installation. I began to get a bit uneasy when, on seeing a great wide muddy river below, I asked the pilot if it was the Rhine. He replied that he didn't know as he was just flying from one radio beacon to another!

Later, we were on our final approach to Paderborn airfield when, about 100 feet up, he suddenly put the aircraft in a 90° bank to the left, with the tops of the trees about 10 feet below our port wing-tip. Anyway, he went round 360 degrees and landed, somewhat shaken, a few minutes later. Before leaving the tarmac, I quietly took aside the guy who was meeting us and asked what had happened. He told me, to my horror, that there had been another aircraft actually landing on the tarmac from the other end of the short single runway as we made our final approach! Apparently, the ground staff had had to fire flares to warn us, as our plane was in the nose-up attitude for landing, and the ex-BA pilot had not seen the other plane, not having bothered to circle the airfield, with which he was obviously not familiar beforehand. I guess this sort of thing doesn't happen much with British Airways at Heathrow.

Much of this book concerns the misdeeds of senior management in large corporations and organisations, such as the Post Office Horizon scandal, and although I have called out many instances of mismanagement, I have not so far suggested any remedies. It is generally true to say that poor decisions that members of management boards or their delegated representatives in middle management take will, sooner or later (unless the organisation is very lucky) adversely and unfairly impact them and their suppliers or, indeed, the organisation's more lowly employees, come back to bite them in the end, and without a change of management style, this is likely to continue unabated.

My proposal would be that a reputable person, say an ex-judge, be appointed to the main board to look after the ethical performance of the (large) organisation and be accessible to outside organisations, e.g. SMEs, as well as employees who feel there is an important issue that is being mishandled by their senior management. The "Director of Ethics" should be able to include a paragraph or two in the company's annual report stating whether ethical problems conformed to the company's Code of Conduct and had been properly dealt with or not. This would be far cheaper and probably far more effective than hiring a PR company to cover up mistakes or, worse still, sweeping them under the carpet, only for them to emerge later with disastrous consequences.

Marketing – when the rubber hits the road

The problem with "Marketing" is that everyone thinks they know what it means – but can't accurately define it. To my mind, it encompasses all sales-related activities – i.e. non-production or administration – that do not actually involve the end-purchaser. Let's start with market research. This aims to discover whether the potential customers will actually buy the new product and the usual approach has been to convene focus groups and ask them what they think of the proposed product or service and whether they personally would buy it.

The difficulty is that, by definition, they would not be there if they were not interested already and there is inevitably some hidden pressure to show some enthusiasm for the product. Again, if the product does not actually exist at that point, perhaps because it is a new concept, will the audience be a good guide as to whether they need/want it? One thinks of chicken and eggs in this context and of Steve Jobs of Apple Computer's remark, "You cannot always wait for the customer to tell you what he wants".

It is a bit easier if the product or service is a new entry into a market that already exists and has similar products available. Then I found that researching market reports on what was already available and how large the market was, and indeed whether it was expanding or not, was quite a good guide as to whether the proposed offering was likely to succeed. For example, Nixdorf Computer wanted to know if their PABX (private telephone exchange) would sell in the UK, so I purchased several market reports from the likes of Frost & Sullivan, specced out what the size of the market was, identified the major players and their products' characteristics, compared those with Nixdorf's PABX, talked to BT, and finished up by writing a report summarising the market potential for a new entry, and specifically Nixdorf's. I also looked at where and why their PABX had already been successful.

After all this, I made a presentation to the senior management at Nixdorf in London, telling them that their product was under-specified compared with the market leaders in the UK, too expensive, too difficult to modify to meet UK public exchange connection requirements, and therefore probably impossible to get connection approval for, and much too late an entry to make a market impact.

I also reported that they had sold it successfully in Germany largely because Nixdorf had a very high profile there and that the German telecoms market was, at that time, not nearly as well developed as in the UK. Even so, the management wanted to go ahead, and it was only because I refused point-blank to be involved in the product's marketing and management that they dropped the idea.

Many years of marketing experience has taught me that a new entry into a developed market almost invariably has to be or be perceived to be either twice as good as the market leader or half the price in order for the customer to be prepared to take the risk inherent in taking on a new product or service. This obviously does not apply to fashion, food or very inexpensive products.

"Good" can obviously mean many things, but usually it has one or more useful features not possessed by the competition. Too often, in my experience, companies, and large companies especially, introduce a me-too type product at only a slightly lower price than the market leader and expect their market clout to make it the new leader. That rarely happens. For example, in the late 1970s, IBM responded to the rising challenge from Digital Equipment Corporation's PDP-11 minicomputers by launching a similar 16-bit mini of their own, called System 1.

This was launched with almost no software and, to the delight of OEM suppliers of systems using PDP-11 machines, such as Arbat, who were battling with IBM in the banking sector, it legitimised the concept of 16-bit minis in the eyes of purchasers – "Mini-computers must be good since IBM's now doing them, but we need proper software, so the System 1 is not for us" – and sales took off for us. It would have been much better for IBM, who were generally regarded as the last word in marketing expertise, not to have entered the minicomputer market at all.

However, the best-laid marketing plans can go completely adrift, as my business partner and I found with our murder mystery game,

Foul Play. It was a multimedia, multi-player version of Cluedo®, designed so that up to six players could play it together, intending to simulate the atmosphere of the famous board game (we **did** have permission from Hasbro) on a multimedia computer. It had lots of Anglicisms in it, for instance, jokes about cricket/baseball, and we assumed that it would do well in the USA and UK, where Cluedo was a market leader.

To our astonishment, it sold several hundreds of thousands of copies in France (in French) and was carried by Virgin, FNAC and Carrefour, amongst other large multiple retailers, but I doubt we sold 100 copies in the UK. We then realised that in the UK especially, computer games were largely played by spotty adolescent boys alone in their bedrooms, whereas in France, a game like this was played by the whole family, or a group of friends, around a table with a glass of wine after dinner.

We should have cottoned on earlier when it proved almost impossible to get the game properly reviewed in the UK by the reviewer playing it with a group of people. Research years later showed that it had been a success in France because the middle/upper-class Anglo lifestyle it portrayed was, and still is, very popular in France.

We had included a single-player option – a bit like playing tennis with a ball-throwing machine – but not surprisingly, this was not as much fun as the multi-player version, resulting in poor reviews as the interplay fun between players was absent. Foul Play also sold well in Australia, perhaps for the same reasons. We still get enthusiastic feedback from the remoter parts of the USA and France, some 30 years after the game was launched.

Befriending the Press can be a great marketing ploy, and when I was at Arbat, I took all the calls from the specialist computer correspondents and especially from Guy Kewney, who regularly resorted to me, probably because he found it hard to get quotes and opinions from the major computer players in the City, such as IBM. As a result, we got far more coverage in the Financial Times than any other computer operation selling to the City. This was a huge advantage and meant that Arbat was much better known than their size or results would warrant.

It did, however, lead to a tricky situation when I was asked to do a write-up of our SWIFT systems for a then reasonably well-known computer industry newsletter called *Datafair* and provide some comment on the rather confused position regarding suppliers of SWIFT interface systems in banks. I had been putting this off for some time as I knew that it would be hard to write an honest appraisal of the situation without offending the SWIFT organisation in Brussels.

The reason for this was that SWIFT had started out by recommending three suppliers: Burroughs, General Automation, and Singer/ICL. Singer/ICL never got their system to work at all and quickly dropped out of the frame. GA did sell about 30 systems, but their software never worked properly (and in due course, all their machines were replaced – often by Arbat), leaving Burroughs as the sole official supplier.

The Burroughs machines, which connected to the Burroughs mainframes doing the message switching in Brussels, were under-powered, unreliable, and could not connect automatically to the bank's own mainframes. They also had poor interfaces for the users, so they were not well-regarded by most of the banks.

Well, under deadline pressure from the *Datafair* newsletter, I wrote this all up and sent it off without checking upstairs, as it was the last day that it could be inserted. I did have the feeling that weekend that I had lit the blue touch paper and retired, and this was confirmed a few days later when the article appeared – and all hell broke loose. Our tubby managing director, Geoff Harris, was summoned to Brussels to explain himself and apologise.

Fortunately, everything I had written was provably true, and though I got a bollocking from him on his return, I was by then able to point out that the Midland Bank, who were one of the biggest users of SWIFT, completely agreed with my comments, at a senior level, and in fact used my article as a lever to expedite a major order to me for a massive SWIFT interface system. This order marked the take-off point for Arbat, as it was the first time a major UK bank had ordered our systems.

When I had visited SWIFT in the World Trade Centre in Brussels sometime before to meet a very nice guy called Peter Drummond, I probed him for information on which banks were using GA systems as I knew that he knew they didn't work and would have to be replaced – ideally by Arbat systems. He produced a listing with the banks' contact names and telephone numbers of all the GA users, and we discussed several of the banks on it, though he did not show it to me and commented that it was confidential.

Inexplicably, he then tore the list in half, dropped it into his wastepaper basket in front of his desk and, excusing himself, left the room. There were one or two other people at their desks in the same open-plan office, but they did not appear to be paying us much attention. Did I retrieve the two halves of the list from his trash and slip them into my open briefcase? Was it a trap? I was myself very torn, but in the end decided that the risk was not worth it.

Probably, Arbat could not, at that time, have delivered working systems to so many banks scattered around Europe without considerable installation help and hardware support from DEC – who, even though Arbat were one of their two largest OEM customers in Europe, were as usual not being co-operative. At least at a corporate level, DEC regarded us as competition in sales to the banks, though they had no banking software at all, and their multi-user operating systems were pretty ineffective.

Also, if I had been caught by one of the other people in the office rummaging in Peter's wastebasket, it would have been very difficult to explain, and indeed, nice though Peter was, it might have been a trap to get Arbat kicked out of the SWIFT environment altogether. In view of the later row about my article, I was quite glad that I had not acted as Peter probably expected me to; I certainly did not need a charge of industrial spying or data theft levelled at me. So – what would you have done in the circumstances – if you were as desperate to get sales as I was in order to feed your family?

Arbat's biggest customer became Barclays Bank. Arbat had been trying to get a deal with them for years until I realised that if we could get SWIFT interface systems into their overseas branches, we could probably expand into handling their banking and accounting systems requirements overseas as well. Fortunately, I got on very well with their guy down in Poole (I had recommended to him a particular club in the Reeperbahn for when he visited their Hamburg branch) who was in charge of SWIFT implementation for their branches and after several solo visits, quoted them a discounted price which would just fit within their budget.

I then went down there by train with Doug Schilling and introduced him as the relevant Arbat director concerned. After some discussion, my contact handed Doug a copy of my letter quoting the price. I was rather apprehensive about this as I knew that Doug would be a bit taken aback, but to give him his due, he concealed his fury with me, and we parted on very good terms with the Barclays man, who told us they would definitely be ordering Arbat SWIFT systems.

The return journey to London on the train with Doug was not very comfortable, but he did have the good grace to say that I had obtained potentially the largest and most important order that Arbat had ever taken. However, on arrival at our offices, I was very soon called in and given yet another rocket by Harris and then another by my line manager, a prat called Geoff Griffiths. The point was that I would never have obtained permission to quote a low enough price to fit Barclay's budget, so there was no point in asking Arbat's management.

The only way to get the order was to set up a fait accompli where Arbat's directors would either have to accept the situation and take the order or walk away – which I knew perfectly well that they would never do.

One of the most significant marketing tools, at least in that era, were brochures or "literature" about the company and its products. The first time I was responsible for this – or rather took on the responsibility myself as I knew no-one else was going to do it – was at Arbat, who up to that point had had no printed brochures at all. I seem to remember taking the excellent advice in Robert Townsend's book "Up the Organisation", which was that brochures with a shiny black cover would not show fingerprints and so would be usable and presentable for much longer than a more traditional white cover. I also came up with a strapline, "Arbat Banking & Communications" or ABC, and got some perspex cubes made with A, B and C in gold letters on three sides and the strapline and Arbat's address on the bottom.

Three of these cubes were stacked up for the cover picture and the whole thing looked neat, clean, original and effective, and we could give out the cubes to actual and potential customers to use as paperweights. There was a hidden joke here as, at that time, IBM gave their customers a Toblerone-like wooden bar for their desks with "THINK" on one side and IBM on the other. It used to really annoy me when I visited an IT (or Data Processing, as they were then called) manager, and he had one of these on his desk, so I like to think that IBM salesmen were equally annoyed when they saw the ABC cube.

Inside the brochure, I chose the famous picture of the rising Earth from the Moon, a picture of the huge satellite dish at Goonhilly Down to symbolise communications, and a picture of our most impressive computer installation and another of specialist trading desks in a Foreign Exchange dealing room equipped by Arbat. The idea being that the Arbat sales team could use these to show what we did – a picture being worth a thousand words. Although I was advised not to do so, I insisted that we use full-page edge-to-edge photographs and place the script on top of the pictures in a contrasting colour, mostly because the picture was far more important than the words.

In fact, the only blurb in the brochure that I did not write went into complete techie-speak and so was not understood by anyone – I suppose then, at least, no one could then dispute it! Naturally no-one at Arbat gave me any credit for the brochure, even though I had designed and produced almost the whole thing, but I was not too concerned because at least I now had a marketing tool that I could really use. I supplemented this with single sheets on particular systems, such as SWIFT and the Intelex message switch.

Exhibitions are also a major marketing tool, and I had some fun at Arbat creating a major exhibition stand at the annual computer communications show in 1980 at the NEC in Birmingham. The idea was to divide the very large stand into two halves, one representing the City of London and the other Wall Street in Manhattan, communicating with each other using our message-switching system.

To aid the impression, we got a lady cartoonist, who was a friend of Jos Roberts, to make a series of street scene drawings of typical views of both cities, including the dome of St. Paul's and a double-decker bus etc. in London and the Empire State building and a fire hydrant for New York. They were line drawings, done with a good sense of scale and a humorous feeling, and when they were blown up to ten feet tall as prints and pasted onto polystyrene panels and clipped onto a light metal framework, they looked terrific. A minor problem was that the 'gulf ' (or Atlantic) between the two halves had to have a small ridge to cover the inter-connecting cables.

During the show, I saw a very annoying Japanese man filming our stand, walking backwards down the gulf and realised that if I didn't stop him, he would trip over the ridge. Well, I didn't, and he did! The stand was not expensive to do and was a huge success, partly because I had read somewhere that most people walk round an exhibition from left to right and our stand was positioned slightly to the left of the front entrance to the exhibition so that people found it convenient to walk through our stand, before visiting any others.

At the opposite extreme and a year or so later, we set up at a much smaller exhibition and were allocated a tiny stand into which we had to fit a minicomputer, two terminals and a printer. In fact, it was so crammed that, with a salesman and a customer or two in it, it looked busier than any of the other stalls in the exhibition and consequently attracted a crowd of curious people craning to see what was going on. Some of whom even bought a system.

Fortunately, these computer exhibitions are now really a thing of the past – even what was the largest in Europe, CeBIT at Hanover, is defunct – since it is possible to show customers pretty much everything via the web or even on your smart mobile, which has a processor far more powerful than any we were using then. In the 1980s and early 1990s, Nixdorf, as the largest computer company in

Germany, had an enormous stand, or rather stands, at CeBIT with hundreds of computers and thousands of terminals on them. In fact the stands were permanent and occupied the same area each year, with a cavernous underfloor bunker holding, at showtime, over 700 minicomputers driving the terminal systems on the stands above.

It was something of a high-stress environment, and indeed, Heinz Nixdorf had a heart attack and died there. I tried to replicate the elements of the relevant system for a banking exhibition in London in the Barbican exhibition area (a converted carpark), but the area we were allocated was not large enough to hold the controlling minicomputers, which were much bulkier than I had anticipated, so they had to be located at our offices in nearby Goswell Road, and the programmers and technicians never really got the software working over the remote telephone link; in all, a nightmare.

So we then reverted to taking customers out to CeBIT, and I particularly remember a trip with some nice guys from the TSB, as the savings bank existed then, before Hill Samuel destroyed it, and then Lloyds Bank submerged it. We had to find accommodation some way outside Hanover as all hotel rooms in and near the city were taken months, if not years, ahead, and I was driving in a hired Mercedes towards Hanover and got completely stuck on the totally jammed autobahn.

After crawling along for half-an-hour and the likelihood of missing the show entirely that day, I spotted a gap in the barriers of the central reservation, just below an overhead bridge. We were going very slowly; there was nothing coming the other way, and we were hidden from police observation on the bridge, so I took the opportunity to sneak through the gap, do a U-turn and head back down the road to a turn-off we had passed ages ago, but just a few miles back.

I thought the TSB guys would be horrified to have their driver do a U-turn on the autobahn, but the senior man in the back just went on reading his book as if nothing had happened, and the others took their lead from him. The typical journey into Hanover was not great, but the only alternative on offer was to stay on a canal boat moored in the city. We did do that one year, but two other customers, returning late after more than sufficient lubrication, fell into the river and had to be fished out – not a happy scene for anyone. I just hoped that the language used was not understood by everyone within earshot.

"It's very user-friendly, when it gets to know you"

When I was at Singer, I had developed, in some quarters, something of a reputation as a Jonah who caused hitherto reliable machines to fail inexplicably. Several years later, I was visiting a stand at a large computer exhibition and was just about to touch the 'Enter' key, as invited to by the display on a computer terminal, when a very loud shout of "Beckett, don't touch that!" made me, and all the nearby spectators, nearly leap out of our skins.

The protester turned out to be a very amusing character who had been with me at Singer, called Bob Brownlee, and who, on recognising me, was determined that I was not going to foul up his precious demonstration. He had had a small and very noisy sports car, which was on one occasion stolen when parked near his house, but after reporting the theft to the police, he told them not to worry about recovering it as it had almost no petrol in the tank, and sure enough he found it abandoned a couple of streets away.

Another character at Singer, Bob Prince, possessed if that is the right word, an ancient minivan with wood fittings in which he accumulated so many parking tickets that the back seats were completely covered in them, to a depth of about a foot. Being temporarily of no fixed address, he left it in a multi-storey car park and went off for a drink or two and forgot where he had left it.

Next morning, he called the police, who duly discovered the vehicle and, having noticed the piles of unpaid tickets, rang Bob and told him that they would not release the car to him until the tickets were all paid. Thinking quickly, he asked the officer to repeat the number plate and, when he did so, told him, "Oh, no, that's not my car." The tickets were worth more than the value of the car!

I noticed another friend at Singer, Gordon Lewis, using a wooden pencil with the inscription – HBLTLOTGWJ – in gold letters. I asked him one day what this meant, to be told that it stood for "Hamish Ben Levis, The Last Of The Great Welsh Jews", which was obviously entirely appropriate as he was neither Welsh nor Jewish. Apparently a friend also at Singer, called David Potts, had given him this joking moniker and the pencils.

Perhaps the most notable and eccentric salesman at Singer was a character called Denis O'Sullivan, for whom the epithet "A legend in his own lunchtime" was, I believe, originally coined in the 1960s. Stories abounded of his ability to get out of even the trickiest sales situations by use of a talent for blarney, unencumbered by even the remotest knowledge of computer systems.

For example, he was being asked a series of questions by a pedantic DP manager about whether the computer he was demonstrating would communicate using IBM 2780 emulation and, 3270 emulation and so on. He had not the vaguest idea what these meant, so having asserted that indeed it coped with all of these (which was more or less true), he noticed some scaffolding out of the window behind the DP manager, with the trade sign "SGB" on it, and with the inspiration of the moment, confirmed that the computer also used SGB 9120 emulation. This completely confounded the DP manager, and he got the sale.

Naturally, his blarney did not work on his wife, the long-suffering Franny, and on one occasion in the middle of winter, when returning late from a dinner in London – reasonably sober, or so he claimed – he found his car parked in the station carpark near his house with the doorlock frozen solid so that he could not get his key into it. Dimly, he remembered that the only way to unfreeze it was to pee on the door lock. He was half way through this performance when a neighbour suddenly appeared to collect his own car parked nearby. The only thing to be done was to stuff everything back into his trousers, with predictable results, so that on arriving home and trying to sneak up the stairs to change his trousers, he was confronted by the redoubtable Franny, who greeted him with "Pissed again, O'Sullivan? You're sleeping on the sofa tonight!"

At about the time I joined Singer, a couple of ex-Army officers were given the task of selling to Insurance Brokers in the City and decided to put on a small playlet for the benefit of their potential customers so that the demonstration started with one of them knocking on the door and being commanded to enter by the other. The new arrival was wearing a bowler hat and carrying a rolled- up copy of the Financial Times under his arm. Accompanied by much banter, he then placed both on the desk, whereupon the FT fell open, revealing a copy of Playboy, and the presentation went on from there. Amazingly, the act was very successful, and the two of them sold quite a few systems, in spite of the fact that the machines were not really powerful enough to do the job nor particularly well-suited for it.

Occasionally you meet someone who would, you suspect, be absolutely ideal for a marketing career, instead of which he is holed up in the technical or computer parts of a bank. One such was a guy called John Fitzgerald who worked at what was then Midland Bank. He was a great tall chap who I met a few times, and he was most amusing, but you would think nothing particularly out of the ordinary.

However, he was a legend at the bank because wherever he went, extraordinary things began to happen. For example, he went into a bar one evening with another banker I knew after visiting the bank's computer operations department in Sheffield. He said to my friend, "Follow my lead. I am going to be Emerson Fittipaldi this evening!" In spite of being six foot five and with only a very passing resemblance to Emmo, who had won the F1 World Championship three or four years previously, he managed to convince everyone in the bar that he was the real thing, and they had a riotous evening with drinks flowing like water – not something you encounter every day in South Yorkshire. There was another evening when he wandered into a party that was being entertained by a hypnotist. Not surprisingly, he volunteered to be one of the subjects being hypnotised, with hilarious results as he turned out to be extremely susceptible to it.

I next met him with a bunch of Midland Bankers in New York a while after and the trip had gone well, as I discovered on my return to the UK, until they were trying to get to the airport to fly back to the UK. There was a taxi and bus strike on in New York, so they were hanging about in the lobby of the Waldorf Astoria discussing what to do when a swarthy guy in chauffeur's uniform and dark shades approached Fitzgerald and said that he was prepared to help, for a consideration, as his boss would not require him for several hours.

Pleased as punch, they all streamed out to his vast black stretch limo – this was at a date when such cars were not at all common, even in New York. They were driving peacefully towards JFK when they heard the sound of police sirens behind them getting louder and louder. Their driver speeded up, and they were soon racing the police cars through New York, with screaming tyres, overtaking in the path of oncoming cars and trucks in traditional NY cop chase style and with disconcertingly abrupt changes of direction.

Inside the car, the bankers all wound up on top of each other on the floor and cowered there, wondering what would happen next. Eventually the limo came to a halt with the sirens blaring all around them as the car was cornered at an intersection. The next thing they heard was the doors being flung open and burly New York cops armed to the teeth commanding them to get out and spread-eagle themselves against the car bonnet and roof.

The 'cuffs were snapped on, and the cops questioned them intently but obviously did not believe their story that they were just Midland bankers from England trying to get to the airport. After a while, with the driver corroborating their story, and with a phone call to the manager of the hotel also supporting it, they were released and given a lift in one of the police cars to the airport.

Apparently, the black limo was the personal vehicle of John Gotti, the Mafia boss, who the police thought was trying to make a break for it.

Consultants – Who Needs Them?

Excluding, naturally, medical consultants and consulting engineers, who are almost invariably extremely well qualified, it is very difficult to see what role the typical management or computer consultant actually plays – do they, for example, know the business better

...then one day I realised people just didn't value my endless, gratuitous, ignorant opinions – so I became a consultant, and charged them for 'em!

than the existing management? Have they actually installed and implemented an identical system in identical circumstances to the one that the IT manager has his eye on?

Robert Townsend's adage that consultants borrow your watch to tell you what time it is and then walk off with the watch still holds good. Selling computer systems in the City was an object lesson for consultants working with banks. Invariably, the bank, large or small, has one of the small number of large firms of accountants doing its auditing and annual accounts.

The accountancy firm will be the first to hear that the bank is looking for a new system and will be delighted to recommend its own computer consultancy operation, which is then called in –

usually at great expense – to advise the bank which system to buy. The computer consultancy would take a cursory look around the market and then recommend IBM – no-one ever got fired for recommending IBM. The bank will then go off and buy whatever hardware and software IBM recommends and the consultants will then have a job for life implementing and maintaining the system.

As I have already indicated, the Arbat systems were greatly superior, much cheaper and far more versatile than any of the small-to-medium IBM systems then in operation and came with ready-made banking software; however, never once in the five years or so that I was selling them did I have a call from any consultants wanting to know more about Arbat's systems.

You would have thought that, if only for curiosity's sake, one or two of them would have wanted to know something about them – if only to shoot them down! What sort of service did the consultants think they were providing for the banks? If there was only one answer, and that was IBM, why were they being employed at, as I said, vast expense anyway?

In fact, we discovered that quite often, the consultants' fees comfortably exceeded the cost of the Arbat system (though probably not the IBM system cost). In recent years, it has become a scandal that the giant accountancy firms have been pushing their consultancy arms onto their corporate customers, often with disastrous results. The problem is that however bright the consultants' people are, they will never know as much about their clients' business as the client does, and really they are being employed as an insurance policy by some – incompetent – managers.

The policy works like this – the manager is too timid to go all out for what he needs and thinks will work, so he asks a consultant in to, in effect, back him up. As it is he who has employed the consultant, the latter will, of course, confirm his view, usually writing a fancy report recommending the very thing that the manager wanted in the first place. Then, if it doesn't work out, the manager can say, "But so-and-so consultants recommended it."

Obviously, the consultants will have anticipated this and either watered down their recommendations or provided enough caveats so that they are still employable by the firm. So, the firm gets a pale reflection of the manager's original idea, which probably will by now (since months will have passed in this process if the consultants have anything to do with it) not work very well, and guess what, the consultants who recommended it will be called in again to set things straight – by which time if he has any sense, the original manager will have moved on.

A large German bank was using what was then called a timeshare system, i.e. they were buying time on a computer service bureau's computer because the volume of their operations in London was, at that point, insufficient to warrant their own machine, and I was called in because they were bankers to and shareholders of Nixdorf Computer, and so they asked me to recommend a system. I proposed a packaged system that we were then selling to small to medium-sized banks, only to be told that it was far too small as they were doing thousands of Foreign Exchange deals per day. I didn't believe their figures and checked with a friend at Citibank who told me that his bank, which was the largest Forex operation in London, was doing fewer than the numbers the German bank was talking about.

In fact, the German bank had only been in operation in London for a few years and was actually doing about a hundred deals a day, which was well within the capacity of our system. The computer service bureau was acting as consultants to the bank and had a vested interest in inflating the figures so that they could sell the bank a system. Nice work if you can get it!

Arbat employed a management consultant who was encouraged to interview members of staff who were unhappy about the operation or direction of the company. I was, therefore, asked to meet this character for an hour or so, and he asked an awful lot of questions – a bit like a therapist –, and I tried to answer them as honestly as possible because he had told me that anything I said would be treated as completely confidential. Big mistake.

I later discovered by chance that he had repeated word-for-word my complaints about several of the senior people at Arbat, who consequently bitterly opposed everything I did afterwards and generally went out of their way to make my life as difficult as possible. In fact, even Arbat realised that the consultant was unusable after this, and I never saw him in their offices again.

Perhaps I am being unfair to consultants, but in 50 years, I have never heard of a consultant doing a really good job for his or her client, whereas I have heard of many ex-

consultants who are now doing something else.

The Government is surely a case in point as it is, apparently, spending £3.5 billion a year of our money on consultants, who are advising it on things that surely only the managers in the departments know anything about, as Government operations are very seldom replicated in the private sector. The enormous IT fiascos perpetrated by the Government in, for example, the National Health Service, are often the result of using consultants, and in that case, the entire system, which I believe cost £20+ billion, was first proposed to Tony Blair by yes, you guessed it, a consultant, who was naturally then put in charge of implementing it! This was not the only IT shambles created by the then-Prime Minister, or by his erstwhile henchman, Gordon Brown, neither of whom are known for their technical expertise.

The Ministry of Defence is rife with consultants, spending about £3 billion on them over 10 years, not to mention numerous ex-military types who never really made the grade in the forces and have been put out to grass there until retirement. In fact, the MoD has managed to completely destroy our hitherto powerful and export-oriented defence industry by consistently prevaricating and procrastinating whenever the critical question of equipment comes up.

As a result, we have been saddled with 232 of the Eurofighter 2000/Typhoon white elephants at a cost of £164 million each, or almost £40 billion in total, whose only purpose is to counter Russian jets. Its ground attack role has only recently (i.e. 15 years after the aircraft was designed) been tacked-on to its mission capability – as evidenced by the complete absence of the jet in Iraq or Afghanistan.

The sensible course would have been to buy F16s at a much lower cost (as the Israelis did), and of course, the F16s have built-in a ground-attack capability, but that would have annoyed our European partners who insisted that Britain buys twice as many aircraft as the RAF can operate – to keep the cost per aircraft down! – with the result that scores of them were mothballed before they were ever used. Finally, even the MoD – or more probably the Treasury – realised the futility of this, and the order has reportedly been scaled back to 160 aircraft, still far more than the RAF can actually use, but apparently, many of the early delivery of aircraft needed replacing, which means that the aircraft has an operational life of only ten years! It will just mean that the RAF can order something even newer and more expensive sooner than they had anticipated.

The situation in armoured vehicles is even worse – and in this case, soldiers have died as a direct result of the failure to provide adequate protection for the driver and occupants. It is absolutely astonishing that anyone at the MoD should ever have felt that Snatch Land Rovers would be in any way adequate in Iraq or Afghanistan to provide protection, firepower or cross-country agility. Alvis, on its own account, had developed a superb small reconnaissance and command vehicle, the Scarab, which had excellent cross-country capability and remotely operated weapons systems (so that the occupants did not have to stand up proud of the vehicle exposing their top halves to enemy fire). It also had thermal imaging for low-light operation and good mine and RPG protection.

Obviously, it was impossible for the MoD to take on such a useful vehicle in the early 2000s, even though the Scarab won competitions against European and US competitors. Far better to remain – at the time – within budget and have 35 or so soldiers die in Snatch Land Rovers (designed for Northern Ireland), be unable to attack the Taliban or insurgents at all in the Snatches, and be unable to go off-road to pursue/avoid the enemy.

The fact that Alvis went under as a direct result and we, i.e. UK taxpayers, had to buy-in US armoured vehicles at unbudgeted (and vast) expense obviously validates the original decision. The MoD even compounded the Snatch fiasco, as if that were possible, by buying similar Jackal open-topped vehicles in which 14 soldiers have already been killed. If those decisions weren't correct, why did nobody own up or resign? No doubt the consultants said that was the route to go, so that's all right then. The Public Accounts Committee, who should have been keeping extravagant spending in check or at least exposing the worst excesses, had the nerve to say that consultants were there to "add value and make improvements that would otherwise not happen". Really?

As if to prove that the Royal Navy is as good at wasting money as the other two services, they have gone and ordered two aircraft carriers that are unable to fly off AWACS aircraft. So this means that the carriers will, for the most part, be motoring about without any idea what is over the horizon (if indeed they are capable of motoring anywhere as they are usually in dock for repair). In other words, we are back to the Napoleonic Wars, or at least the Falklands in 1982, when we were extremely lucky not to have HMS Invincible sunk by an Exocet fired from about 20 miles away, which in the last seconds diverted automatically to sink the larger target of the Atlantic Conveyor. The aircraft carrying the Exocet was not visible on the ship's radar as it was over the horizon.

We had no AWACS at sea then, and we will have none now. The really sad thing is that, by accident, we had the perfect ship, HMS Ocean, the helicopter carrier, to perform all sorts of useful and beneficial tasks, such as search and rescue, disaster relief, anti-terrorist operations, etc., but of course it was cheap, and nobody's career is going to take an upward trend in Nelson's Navy by commanding such a commonplace ship, whose hull was built using cheap cargo ship methods.

Naturally, the Royal Navy only had one, when what we want, obviously, is purpose-built (i.e. expensive) pointy ships like the Type-45 Destroyers, with their single (!) helicopter, plus indefensible white elephants like the new carriers, all taking years to complete, at vast expense.

It has to be said that the RAF is the same, opting for fast pointy aircraft like the Typhoon rather than useful aircraft like the Spectre used by the US Special Forces, basically a (cheap) C-130 propeller-driven transport aircraft fitted with side-firing, trainable 25mm, 40mm, and 105mm guns. The strike radar provides the first gunship capability for all weather/night target acquisition and strike. Useful in Afghanistan, where our armed forces were committed for at least ten years? Yes, I think so, but no-one is going to get promoted flying safely round and round at 15,000 feet, supporting the Army – oh please! Much better to spend £164 million – per aircraft – of other people's money on something that is super fast. Alternatively, they could have bought the A10 Warthog, a heavily armoured, sub-sonic, highly effective ground attack aircraft favoured by the Israelis.

I could go on and on about the polyhedron of procurement failures (the MoD even have the nerve to call it "Smart Procurement", a term no doubt dreamt up by a consultant – heaven knows what "dumb (or normal) procurement" would bring!) which include the helicopter fiascos, both Merlin and Chinook, MR3 Nimrod, Sea Dart missile, Bowman radios, dust filters (or lack of them) for Challenger tanks in Iraq, porous boots that gave 15% of the infantry trench foot in the Falklands, the SA80 (before it was modified) rifle fiasco, to name but a few.

In fact, it is very hard to recall any procurement successes driven by the MOD, as opposed to product initiatives from armaments suppliers like Alvis, where the item ordered actually arrived on time and on budget – and worked properly the first time! Naturally, the MoD had to have a facility (Abbeywood, Bristol), seemingly rather larger than the Pentagon, to do all this procurement from, and yes, you guessed right, it features lakes, fountains, atriums, fancy glass, internal "streets", plus a moat with a bridge over it! Cost = £174 million. Oh, and most of the staff there get an annual bonus for procuring – what? – so successfully.

It is easy to throw rocks at consultants, and I acted as one for a while, during which time I achieved precisely nothing whilst being paid to give advice to all and sundry on "Multimedia". The problem is that consultants seldom actually **do** anything. They are called in to help with whatever project but are rarely, if ever, given a brief that says, "Do this, by such-and-such a time, at such-and-such cost."

Their role is to sort of come up with a brief, so they suggest this and suggest that, confident in the knowledge that if the client adheres to their advice, and it doesn't work (i.e. usually), they will have plenty of opportunities to 'adjust' their brief in the meantime. Anyway, if the project is at all complex – and why did you want them if it wasn't? – it will take time to put into effect, so they will have moved on long before the shit hits the fan. Consultancy is the epitome of "power without responsibility – the prerogative of the harlot throughout the ages", as Rudyard Kipling had it. Recent figures show that the number of consultants is actually falling, so maybe the business world is getting the message, though obviously not the Government.

Management – Seeing the Wood from the Trees?

It has been said (by Robert Townsend) that "Top Management", far from being able to tell the wood from the trees, is frequently not even sure where the forest is, and in my experience, most good ideas are generated well below the level of

"OK. I admit it, we're lost, but the important thing is to remain focussed on whose fault it is."

top management, who are normally more concerned with what they regard as keeping the show on the road, for example ensuring that the books balance and that the bank and the investors/shareholders are happy.

Top management rarely takes the time to walk around the place and see what is going on. Much better to stay in its office or out at play rather than meddle with the workings of the operation. In all the offices I have worked in, I don't believe that I **ever** saw **any** of the management (with the sole exception of Doug Schilling) just walking around, seeing what was going on, talking to people about their problems, suggesting solutions and generally making people feel wanted and useful. Yes, certainly, senior managers turned up for meetings – usually called by them – but almost never did I see or hear a manager go walkabout around his or her own offices. Why not?

I guess there are two main reasons. Firstly, most managers are not capable of doing most of the things that their subordinates are capable of doing, and so they are nervous about being made to appear stupid or ignorant by asking questions or making comments. Alternatively, they are too stupid or lazy to take the trouble to check out their own operations and prefer to rely on people to do their job and report back in writing (so they can be fired if things go wrong).

At Arbat, during the development of the message switching and electronic mail systems that I designed, I walked around the desks of the guys who were actually doing the coding and asked them how it was going. Had they got room to fit this or that data field in, what length they were making the fields, etc., etc? I was heavily criticised for doing this by – senior management – but the net result was that the programmers allowed for all the fields in the addressing database that were needed to turn a message switch into an e-mail system.

If I had just sat back and hoped they would put in the facilities an e-mail system needed, they would never have bothered. In fact, at the outset of the message switch development I was asked by Roger Worthington, the head of development, to provide the software team with a flow chart defining the design of the system. Realising that the requirement centred on an effective queuing system, I went out and bought the definitive book on queuing theory, read it over the weekend and drew the flowchart on one A4 sheet, completing it on the following Monday. Roger's only comment was, "You haven't identified where the last box connects to." Obviously, it connected to the first, as it was an iterative process.

In spite of this, I was accused of meddling in the development and told to stay out of it. Naturally, I ignored this, which caused more trouble. Ironically, I heard an interview with one of the founders of Gore Associates in which he was asked what he actually did, and he replied, "Well, I suppose you could call it meddling; I walk around asking questions, discussing problems and making suggestions". I guess this is also easier without some pompous title, such as Vice-President, or Director of Human Resources or whatever.

I have always taken the view that, as a manager or leader, you should never ask anyone to do anything that you cannot do yourself. Your guys may be able to do it faster or better than you can because they have more practice at that task, but you **should** be able to perform the task. For example, it was thought impossible for managers to do their own typing, so armies of secretaries, i.e. typists, were employed to type letters and reports. Strange how almost everyone does their own typing nowadays – but how else would you handle your own e-mails?

The Army was a good model for self-proficiency in that all of us, officers and men, were taught basic infantry skills before anything else, and then taught how to drive and maintain tanks, how to shoot their guns and use their radios – in addition to learning about leadership and tactics. These were a far more complex set of skills than are usually required in an office and naturally took time to acquire and become proficient at.

One of the main reasons I left the Army was that under the then Labour Government in the late 1960s, we were only allowed (for cost reasons) to drive our tanks for 67 miles a year. It is quite impossible to train an army with that little mileage – roughly equivalent to one day's motoring in a tank.

Luckily, after several years in tanks, I was given the command of Reconnaissance Troop, which had wheeled Scout Cars (Ferrets) to which this mileage restriction did not apply, and on the first available opportunity, I spent ten days doing 'Tiger' training in which the object was for two cars to capture a single one by positioning themselves fore and aft of it. This required considerable map-reading, tactical, command and driving skills to be successful – and was enormous fun as well. As a result, when we went out on a major exercise a few months later, the troop was told by the commanding officer of the 4th Tank Regiment – the then-professional Recce regiment in Germany – that we were the best Recce Troop he had ever seen. A further bonus was that the drivers were properly trained and didn't overturn any of the Ferrets, something that happened under the command of almost all of my predecessors and, I believe, most of my successors.

Fortune favoured me on that exercise in a rather unlikely way in that, instead of the Land Rover I would normally have used, I was given a 'Field Mouse', which was a Ferret without the machine gun turret, because the troop Land Rover was being used by my Squadron-Leader, Major Ashford-Sandford, to carry poles to erect a hunter trial course near Osnabruck. Though completely open to the elements, the Field Mouse was much lighter than the normal Ferret and, in fact, had probably the best power-to-weight ratio of any vehicle in the Army.

The exercise area was in the mountainous area near Wuppertal, Germany and needless to say it rained continuously for the whole of the five-day exercise. This meant that the command vehicles of the two squadrons that I was attached to could not get up the muddy forest tracks and so had to stick to the roads at the foot of the hills, with the result that they could not get good radio communications to their troops or Headquarters.

Being able to shimmy my way up on top of the steep hills I could hear what was going on and started by relaying messages between the various troop and squadron-leaders. On the second day of the exercise, one of my own section leaders crept up on an "Orders Group" being held by the 'enemy' squadron and gathered most of what was planned by them. He radioed this on to me on my own troop net and I realised that I could anticipate most of the enemy moves and cut them off.

I, therefore, began by making suggestions for the deployment of the rest of the squadrons 'fighting' on our side, and these were so successful that I virtually took over the command of the two squadrons, as well as my own troop. A bit unusual, to say the least, for a Lieutenant to command the equivalent of a regiment on exercise! It was great fun but totally exhausting as we were operating in appalling weather all day up to nightfall, the aim being to simulate battlefield conditions.

In fact, sitting all day and some of the night in an open scout car with minimal protection from the wind and rain, wearing semi-waterproof clothing at best, poring over my plastic-covered map with the regimental net coming in one earphone and my troop net in the other, while all the time directing my driver was, to say the least, an intellectual challenge of the first water. I found that after concentrating so hard on a relatively small area on the Ordinance Survey-type maps we were using, I was able to form a realistic 3-D image of the ground we were passing over from the map in my head.

This was incredibly useful as it became possible to visualise the ground from different points of view, principally the 'enemies' and ours, to identify whether we could see them from a particular viewpoint/location before they saw us. Apparently the latest 'Smart

Soldier' equipment carried by the soldier of tomorrow (if the project is not cancelled by the MoD) provides the same facility!

It may be said that I should have passed the intelligence on up the line of command, but there was great rivalry between the Tank Regiments and the Cavalry regiments – the latter being regarded as amateurs by the Tankies – and I was keen to put one over on them. What I learnt on that exercise was that it was imperative to give exact orders – taking into account the ground as well as our, and the enemy's, dispositions – to the section leaders in my troop so they knew their exact objectives – and then let them get on with it.

Only they could assess the precise conditions of their own situation and act accordingly, but they had to conform to the overall plan dictated by me. They were all intelligent guys, specially picked for the job and got the point, so it worked really well. Is this management approach very different from best practices in business or industry today? At that date, however, this was revolutionary stuff in an Army still dedicated to a hierarchical top-down approach and which prided itself in giving orders for every little eventuality, with no initiative required or called for, from the lower ranks.

In fact, it was only with the advent a few years later of the troubles in Northern Ireland that the Army realised that it was imperative to allow junior leaders scope for initiative. My squadron leader, nick-named Ashcan, did not approve, needless to say, and used a tiny flaw – a nail found in a tyre that a scout car picked up on its way to the inspection area – in my troop's 'important' annual mechanical inspection, to get rid of me.

However, before I left Recce I was due to go out on a patrol of the border with East Germany, as it was then at the height of the Cold War, and had everything planned for the start date in the middle of the week. I was suddenly told by the adjutant on Saturday that I had to leave the next day as the patrol had been brought forward to Monday morning.

Chaos ensued as I tried to get everything together and also make arrangements to meet my girlfriend, Virginia, who was visiting me that weekend and to whom I was by then secretly engaged, at the town of Duderstadt on the East-West German border, where we were to be based for the patrol. The 200km journey was a nightmare with bad visibility, frequent traffic diversions (common in Germany on Sundays) and several breakdowns, meaning that we had to abandon the 3-ton supplies truck, with its driver, in the middle of nowhere.

Virginia and I met up late on Sunday night after a very difficult journey for her, too, and I called the man who guided us for the border patrols the following morning. He was very surprised to hear from me as he was not expecting me for another two days. Luckily, I did not mention that we were already at Duderstadt, just 1km from the border, as he warned me that arriving early in military vehicles would be a serious contravention of the treaty with East Germany.

So we laid low in the town for a couple of days before commencing the patrol on the original date. In the process of driving along close to the actual border, we came across a well-worn path crossing through the wire and the minefields on the East side of the border, and our guide stopped and ordered me to load live ammunition. Of course, we did not have any, as it had been impossible to draw it out from the secure ammo dump on a Sunday. Anyway, we did our best to pretend to load the machine guns, and luckily, no one opened fire on us.

So why had I been sent out three days early? The adjutant at the time was a very chippy little man called Nash, who I think resented my having a girlfriend out to visit me, and so decided to send me off on patrol early. Actually, he did me a favour as I got to spend not just the original weekend but another five days with Virginia in a beautiful part of Germany. When I got back to camp, I should have caused a huge row and got Nash fired – if not court-martialled – which would have done everyone a favour as he eventually greased his way up to be a thoroughly objectionable commanding officer, however in the first flush of love I didn't really care.

After Recce Troop, I was assigned to the command of Headquarters Troop with a variety of interesting vehicles including the regiment's only bridge-laying tank, a bulldozer and various command and communications vehicles. Needless to say, I had a great deal of fun with these on exercise and was probably the first troop leader in my regiment interested enough to test out all their capabilities, including the explosive bolts, which, when fired from inside the bridge layer, released the bridge from its shackles without anyone leaving the safety of the interior of the armoured vehicle, so that the bridge could be laid across a river. A senior officer was watching this when the bolt whistled past his head – I was advised not to do that again.

All of these vehicles, plus the Recce Troop vehicles, were crammed into a single tank hangar, which, unlike the other tank hangars, had a wall across part of its entrance, making it even more difficult to get vehicles in and out. I protested many times about this to my squadron leader and to anyone else, including the adjutant, the colonel, the quarter-master, etc., as it was clearly very dangerous, particularly if there was a fire in the hangar.

I even discovered that there were indeed several empty hangars – one of which contained the Technical QMs personal caravan sitting there in a solitary and empty state. I moved the bridge-layer, it being the largest vehicle, out into another hangar but was ordered by my squadron leader to put it back. I even asked to do a fire practice to see what would happen, but was forbidden to do so – as it was too dangerous! In due course, my worst fears were realised.

One Saturday morning, I had been asked to look after a potential new officer recruit and was showing him round when I got a call from the tank park saying an accident had happened. I rushed down there and found one of my troopers, a rather sad character called McGuigan, lying on the ground, soaked in blood. He had been crushed against the protruding wall on the corner of the entrance by a vehicle exiting from the hangar – exactly as I had predicted. He was taken to hospital with a caved-in chest and horrendous internal organ damage.

While I was waiting at the hospital to hear the result of the operation, I got a call from my squadron leader blaming **me** for the accident! I was completely shocked and absolutely furious, but before I could formally complain had to race off to collect the dying trooper's mother from the airport and look after her for a day or two until the funeral. She was absolutely distraught about her only child being killed as she was now completely alone, his father having left her some years previously. I was then more than a little surprised to find that I had been ordered to act as second-in-command of another squadron, which was departing immediately for an exercise in France – presumably so that I could not give evidence at the enquiry.

Obviously, I had a duty of loyalty to my regiment, of which I was extremely proud, and was anyway leaving the Army in a few weeks' time, but as far as I know, my squadron leader never came before a court-martial, as one would expect, though he **was** farmed out on some extra-regimental duty in England as a passed-over major until he could be retired. I had an extraordinary letter, addressed to me personally, many years after I had left the Army, which asked if I knew of any instance where a soldier who was homosexual had been discriminated against. If someone, somewhere did not know of this case, why contact me?

Another incident which confirmed my desire to leave the Army showed just how stupidly the Army could act. There was a major problem with the command vehicle in my HQ troop because the radios in the vehicle created tremendous static electricity, which could not be released in dry conditions on roads because they had rubber pads on their tracks to minimise damage to the tarmac.

The static build-up meant that radio communications were very badly affected, particularly whilst the vehicle was on the move by road, i.e. most of the time while on exercise. I had noticed that German cars often had, at that time, a metal strap hanging down from their underside, and on asking a local garage, they confirmed that this was to eliminate static. I, therefore, got someone to weld some army standard-issue metal lavatory chains to the underside of the command vehicle.

This completely solved the static problem, but not long afterwards, I was ordered by my squadron leader to remove them permanently as the vehicles were due to be inspected, and this was not an official modification. The fact that two large metal 'coffin bins' normally attached to the turret of a tank had been welded to the top of the same command vehicle so that they could contain the colonel's personal kit mattered not a jot.

On my final exercise in the army, my troop was combined with one of the very few Armoured Engineers troops which had some truly impressive machinery, such as a massive bulldozer tank with a 165mm gun which fired a dustbin-sized explosive shell for blasting down bridges or obstructions. The troop also possessed a tank that pulled a huge two-wheeled trailer carrying a rolled-up aluminium and steel roadway and/or some fascines, or large bundles of brushwood, for filling in ditches.

My opposite number, the Armoured Engineer troop leader, chose this enormous contraption as his personal command vehicle and managed to get it completely stuck down a very muddy and steep ramp to a previously dug-in tank firing position.

He was unable to back it out and was stuck there for three days, during which I had a marvellous time with all his vehicles, supported by his troop Sergeant who clearly thought he was a complete prat and had no desire to rescue him, even if we could. Every now and then, I received a pathetic bleat over the radio, which naturally I ignored or pretended that radio static was too bad to hear properly, as there were far more important, or at any rate, interesting, things to do.

The good part about the Army was the incredibly high calibre of the best NCOs and (almost) all of the Warrant Officers, and it has to be said that, in reality, it was on them that the Army depended because of their experience and not least, their great sense of perspective and humour. You offended them at your peril, but if they were on your side, almost anything became possible. If the Army had to rely entirely on its officers, heaven knows what would happen.

Occasionally, in business, you do find the equivalent of the best NCOs, but almost never a Sergeant-Major, though that role was, for many years, filled by matrons in the NHS, for example. I was lucky enough to work with a couple of guys, one at Arbat, Mike Evans, and one at Virgin, Steve Clarke, who filled the role of very senior Sergeants or Sergeant-Majors and were terrific to work with.

Their knowledge and experience was invaluable, and without their hard work and intelligence, I would have been completely lost. Never mind about them saluting me; it was a case of me saluting them! So why do you need officers if you have guys like these? Well, the short answer is that officers are expendable leading their troops, whereas NCOs and WOs are not. However, as senior officers in a company become less and less inclined to take real responsibility, i.e. if their whole project doesn't work, to accept the blame and resign, the buck is passed down to the real core of the company, who are then blamed and shamed.

This is completely self-defeating because, without those people and their experience and expertise, the company is nothing. But what usually happens is that nobody takes responsibility – though, of course, "lessons are learnt". The reality is that unless the person responsible is fired or moved on, the whole organisation degrades, the best people see no future for themselves and leave, and a downward spiral commences.

The final denouement of my time in the Army was in a meeting of all the officers in the regiment, which had been called so that General, later Field-Marshal, Michael Carver, the General Officer in Southern Command and the Army's top tank expert, could explain to us why it was so important that there was a BAOR or British Army of the Rhine. He expanded for half an hour on how important our role was in defending Western Europe against possible Soviet aggression and then asked questions.

Earlier that year (1968), it had been announced that the latest British tank, the Chieftain, had been sold to Persia, which was then ruled by the Shah, who had ordered 400 Chieftains at a cost of £400m and was taking priority in delivery over the British Army. I, therefore, asked the General why, if our job was so vital, were we not getting priority delivery of the Chieftain, as our Centurion tanks were of WWII vintage and consequently very unreliable, being fitted with WWII Merlin high maintenance petrol engines? He looked really pissed off with me and waffled something about budgets and priorities before quickly winding up the meeting.

Afterwards, my commanding officer came up to me and said, "Well done, William. That was the question we were all dying to ask. Probably just as well that you are leaving the Army, though!" Mind you, even 400 Chieftains would probably not have delayed for more than a few days an invasion from the East, where 5,000 tanks were waiting just over the border. Indeed, that same year, 2,000 of them invaded Czechoslovakia in the Prague Spring repression.

Those Chieftain tanks, though already paid for, experienced endless production delays and were never delivered to Iran as a result of the UK Government's change in attitude to that country after the revolution there when the Shah was deposed. So, when they were finally ready to ship, the Government's military sales organisation had secured an order from Saddam Hussein, so they went to him and were paid for again!

Saddam used them to help him invade Iran, resulting in over 1 million deaths. Some years later, Iran started demanding their money back and sent over two government representatives, one of whom was smartly returned to Tehran, and the other locked up, though later released.

The UK Government were eventually forced to repay Iran when they demanded the money in exchange for releasing a hostage – Nazanin Zaghari-Ratcliffe. No wonder our name in the Middle East is mud.

Multimedia – Its Birth And My Part In It

I had long thought that computers would not realise their full potential until they handled colour graphics, pictures, video and audio, as well as text, and I helped kick this idea into action by specifying a 20" colour graphics screen to show the manager of the message switching system installation what was going on at a glance – and obviously to make it more appealing

when selling the system. In fact at that date, 1978/9, these were some of the very first colour graphics screens sold anywhere and were pretty expensive at about £2,000 each.

I used the limited range of eight colours to define some of the telegraph/telex lines as receiving messages, some as transmitting them and other colours to show errors, or lines not in use etc. Stock Exchange screens now use a similar approach to show share prices rising (in blue) and falling (in red). As usual, I got a lot of flack from people at Arbat for proposing such an outlandish idea, but after we began installing the systems, I proposed not to include a colour screen in a tender for one prospect in order to reduce our price, only to be told that the system would not work without it!

Whilst at Nixdorf in the mid-1980s I met a guy called Terry Clarkson who was involved in Interactive Video, which was what later became known as Multimedia, and who had (with quite a few others) seen the potential to use it for industrial training. The systems were relatively expensive, often costing £5,000 or more, and comprised a PC with a special Printed Circuit Card linking it to an industrial-quality videodisc player.

Pre-CD-ROM this was the only way that multimedia could be produced and all sorts of people with widely differing agendas leapt on what they fondly imagined was the bandwagon. Industrial Training was one of the only viable applications, and Terry and I formed what was, in effect, a UK offshoot of The Industrial Training Corporation based in Washington, DC. We persuaded the Americans to make a programme on Statistical Process Control (SPC), the continuous-improvement-of-process methodology for making better products using statistical analysis to eliminate causes of deviation from the norm. They agreed, on the condition that we found suitable sites for filming in the UK and looked after their film crew when they were over here. The crew did a terrific job but insisted on filming in the American-standard NTSC system, as all their filming and editing gear was oriented around that.

We had an amazing time on the various shop floors and saw some appalling practices in action. For example, at Jaguar, there was a wall full of long racks at one end of the production line, three levels high, laden with scores of completed engines that had failed their bench tests. This meant that they all had to be scrapped, but it also meant that the quality control of the parts that made up the engines was deficient – an appalling waste.

At Land Rover we saw a guy standing at the machine that turned crankshafts, start up the machine and produce the first one. He then took one he had turned earlier out from under his bench, went through the motions of measuring it for tolerance and put it back under the bench. He then placed the recently made crankshaft into the "parts completed and checked bin" and continued on his way. The point was that the machine, when started up, would not produce the first part within tolerance, but, as he was on piecework, every part counted towards his pay.

We also visited Ransomes, who made ball-bearings, which is an incredibly complex process, and were able to see the completed ball bearings drop into a tray with multiple different-sized divisions, having been automatically measured for size. As intended, the majority of the balls were in the centre of a standard distribution, producing a beautiful example of a bell curve in action.

We were delighted with this visual confirmation of statistical analysis of parts production, but, on asking Ransomes about it, they unaccountably became angry and even abusive, as they thought we were taking the piss out of their quality control, so something very odd was going on. We never found out what, but as they had signed off, giving us permission to film and use the output, we realised that it was better to beat a hasty retreat with the film already in the can.

We attempted to convert the resulting NTSC – 30 frames to the second material – to the British PAL 25 frames per second system, but it did not work properly as the two systems were incompatible for interactive video purposes, both in the number of images per second and also the image frame which meant that what was perfectly shot on NTSC was missing parts of the picture when converted to, what was in effect, the different frame size of PAL. However, the programmes were a great success in the USA and were sold to Ford and then many other manufacturers. In due course, the SPC message got back across the Atlantic, and Britain now enjoys some of the highest-quality production in the world. I am proud of the admittedly small part I played in that revolution.

In the 1980s, colour screens began to appear on home micros such as the BBC micro, and the emergence of the BBC Domesday system, which linked an adapted BBC micro to a videodisc player, became one of the first multimedia systems that were not purpose-built for a specific customer. The idea of the BBC Multimedia Group was to get these into schools in the UK and after the two Domesday discs, which were sold with the system, produce other discs to take advantage of the system's multimedia capabilities. The Domesday discs included information on a wide range of subjects from sources all over Britain and included maps, archives, etc., to present a modern-day Domesday Book, with much of the data collected by volunteers, including many schools.

Mindstorms: Children, Computers, and Powerful Ideas was a very influential book on learning theory written by Seymour Papert of MiT in collaboration with Jean Piaget. It came out in 1980 and advocated a constructionist approach to education – learning by doing. Papert and Piaget advocated using computers in class to provide environments that were otherwise impossible for children to explore, specifically in mathematics, but also in social interaction.

They felt that the teaching of maths should start in kindergarten by letting children loose on computers to build simple robots, for example, and then later on learn the formal 'grammar' of maths because 90% of the maths taught in school is of no use at all in later life, they say it is about how numbers are written, rather than understanding them. Interestingly girls proved to make much more useful machines than boys who just want their machine to go faster and further than anyone else's – and preferably to smash the others' up! For example, Papert cites one case where a girl wanted to make a machine to dance with.

I took this concept on board and decided to create a multi-user, multimedia experience based on Sir Ranulph Fiennes' Transglobe

Expedition, taking advantage of the BBC Domesday machine's videodisc to hold the video, audio and pictures, and its trackball (an upside-down mouse) being able to be passed around among a group of six children, each taking on the role of expedition leader, pilot, medic, navigator, mechanic and base commander respectively.

The programme mimicked a journey across the icepack to the North Pole and was a race against time to get to the Pole and then meet their ship before the icepack broke up in the Spring, with the children having to make the right decisions to overcome the problems and disasters that the real expedition had encountered.

Following Papert's precepts, this environment was something that none of the children (nor their teacher) had ever encountered before, so everyone started on a level playing field/ice floe, and it was fascinating to observe the class know-all/computer nerd/bully come unstuck when faced with situations he had never been in before and be put in his place by a thoughtful little girl, for example.

Apart from learning about the Polar environment, which even then was of increasing importance, the programme simulated the use of a theodolite to 'shoot the sun' to calculate your position – an interesting use of maths in the real world. The programme was highly popular with children but less so with teachers who found it difficult to integrate it with their lesson plans in an increasingly prescriptive educational system.

A further problem was that the BBC Domesday system was unwieldy, to say the least, with numerous wires and plugs and consequently somewhat daunting to put together, so it tended to reside in the school library rather than the classroom, and the noise and excitement that the North Polar Expedition (NPE) programme generated in the children was barely containable in the classroom, never mind the hushed atmosphere of the library.

In fact, I was told that the main problem in one school – King Edward VI's in Birmingham – was that the watching children not playing one of the prescribed roles got so excited that they leapt on the desks and shouted and cheered the expedition players on! I guess partly because the BBC Domesday system cost £3,000, the take-up of the system in schools was much less than expected, with probably less than 800 units sold in all, some of which never made it out of the computer cupboard, so our sales of about 350 units of NPE (@£199) was not too bad in the circumstances.

Were lessons learnt? Well, yes, the main lesson obviously was that multimedia development should only proceed on mainstream platforms, such as the PC, or if that was impossible because the PC was at the time such a feeble multimedia platform, then development must be subsidised by the relevant manufacturer of multimedia-capable devices, such as Commodore or Philips.

In fact, it was almost impossible to display images in anything like reasonable resolution on a PC screen without a special card and videodisc player in 1989/1990, but I heard of some people near Washington DC who had found a way using a little-known facility called Mode 8. I persuaded them to convert the NPE programme to CD-ROM – with modifications, as there was no sound card then in use on the PC – to run in that environment. It was a little tricky, to say the least, because the PC at that time had an addressable memory of 640 Kbytes and no virtual memory on disc, so the operating system **and** the NPE programme had to run in less than 640K, and actually it took 625K, which meant some normal PC functions had to be turned off. But, hey, NPE was probably the very first multimedia programme to run on a PC and be sold to the general public.

It was delivered on a CD-ROM, and I went to meet the IBM people in Basingstoke who were responsible for marketing the PC (other manufacturers not having yet ramped up production) to ask them what plans they had for their PC and CD-ROM drives and whether they might ship NPE as a promotional programme with the drive. To my amazement they denied that they even sold a CD-ROM drive and were not best pleased when I pointed one out in their catalogue. Not a very productive morning.

Before moving on I would like to mention a couple of stories about Ran which go a long way to illustrate his character – and which, being the charming and unassuming character he is – he would never include in his excellent and entertaining books. The first was while we were at Eton, and as Ran has written in his autobiography, he took up boxing to get away from the 'pretty boy' image that he had unwittingly and unwillingly acquired. In one match in the annual school boxing competition, he was put up against Daniel Meinertzhagen, for whom I fagged[4] and who was, to say the least, something of a bully, as well as being, up to that point, the school boxing champion at his weight.

Ran, though quite tall, was considerably lighter, younger and a less experienced boxer than Meinertzhagen, so it was a very popular win, not least with me, when he stopped Meinertzhagen in the third round. The next was told me by a mutual friend at Eton, who had skived off to the cinema in Slough in "change clothes" during a period when there had been considerable friction with the local youths in Slough, who had duffed up one or two Etonians.

This fellow, Duckworth, was keeping a low profile near the back row of the cinema when he heard the doors behind swing open and, glancing back, saw what seemed to him like a huge figure in black leather, gloves and motorbike helmet, clump down the steps towards him. Trying to make himself as small and inconspicuous as possible in his seat, he was terrified to get a thump on the shoulder, there was an ominous pause, and then he heard a familiar voice say, "Hello Duckworth, what the fuck are you doing here?" Ran, needless to

---

4 The abused and discredited system then in place of forcing younger boys to run errands for the senior boys

say, had found a way of acquiring and keeping a motorbike hidden near the school.

Perhaps more relevant is an incident, given Ran's subsequent expeditions to both Arctic and Antarctic, which took place during the annual ski competitions in Oberjoch in Southern Germany. Ran was there to langlauf for his regiment, whilst I did both the langlauf and downhill for mine. He had arrived in a three-ton truck with his soldiers and had succeeded, much to everyone's envy, in asking the very pretty captain, who was leading the WRNS's team, out to dinner.

Ran's reputation as a fairly scary and fearless driver was already pretty well known, so, finding no-one to lend him their car, he 'borrowed' the regimental three-ton truck, but not wanting to be seen by any senior officers, headed across the nearby Austrian border, which fortunately was not manned at night.

On the way back, the close proximity in the cab overcame them both, apparently, and a temporary stop in a lay-by was called for while they repaired to the back of the vehicle where honour (or something) was satisfied on the bare metal floor of the lorry. Clearly, this was a happy outcome for all concerned, judging by the expression on the lady captain's face the next day, though the smile was somewhat diminished when, during her race, she was obstructed from going through a gate by my fiancée, who was stuck sideways in it, and both of them disqualified. I knew that Ran would have no worries about frostbite travelling across the coldest parts of the Earth if he could manage it in pitch darkness on the bare metal floor of an Army lorry at -25°C!

Fortunately, I was able to use the marketing clout of Virgin to persuade Commodore, who had been very successful with their Amiga games micro but now were marketing their new CDTV multimedia system and wanted brand name partners, to put in quite a lot of money to convert NPE to the CDTV platform.

Unfortunately, the rather laid-back guy who was doing the conversion at Virgin took so long over it that we missed the peak sales moment, and I could do little about it because, by that time, I had left Virgin and was just acting as a consultant for them. The other multimedia programme that we produced at Virgin was a music teaching programme called Musicolor, based on the teachings of the late Candida Tobin, and using, as the name suggests, a colour system to help children learn to understand, remember and read music.

She was an extremely charismatic teacher who had designed and developed her system and sold it quite widely to schools in England. The challenge was to produce a system that got all her principles across whilst retaining the charm and enthusiasm that she imparted when teaching in person. The programme, which ran on CDTV, was neat and effective and I think did to some extent achieve that very ambitious objective, in so far as it was actually achievable. However, it sank with the demise of the CDTV system.

NPE and Musicolor were ground-breaking programmes well ahead of their time, and the principles they used were defined as de facto educational archetypes in a mid-2000s article in the Daily Telegraph by Professor Stephen Heppell, founder of the Ultralab at Anglia Polytechnic University, and named Europe's leading ICT education expert.

I used videodisc in an experimental arcade-type game that Steve Clark and I developed at Virgin to simulate an interactive ride on the famous Cresta Run at St. Moritz, using a concept vouchsafed to me by William Donelson who had produced an underground garage parking simulator using videodisc that he showed me. We filmed it with three cameras on a specially built sledge that we lowered down the Run itself, taking shots with each camera at intervals of a few inches at the Top when the rider has yet to pick up speed, increasing to a yard and a half or more at the Finish which, when played back continuously, simulated gradual progression to over 90 miles an hour.

Unfortunately the videodisc player would not jump 100% of the time over the two or more frames between each frame it needed to use and tended to lock up after a few runs. It wound up in Washington, DC, as the centrepiece of a multimedia exposition. We did try it with several experienced Cresta riders, who were virtually climbing the walls with excitement as they navigated down the Run. They said that they saw things in the game that they never saw in real-life runs on the Cresta.

The multi-user approach of NPE was used again to good effect in the next major project I undertook with two guys, Peter Deutsch and Jon Baldachin, whom I had met previously at Virgin. They had secured the digital rights from Waddingtons to a number of brand name games such as Monopoly, Risk and Scrabble, which were converted to computer versions with reasonable success.

They suggested to me in 1993 that I use some of the same 'Virtual Travel' technology that I had used on the Cresta Run game to produce a multimedia version of Cluedo®. I again contacted William Donelson, who I had met when he was producing industrial training interactive video discs for the North Sea oil industry.

These ground-breaking programmes used a technique he had worked on ten years earlier at MiT in the Aspen, Colorado, project to simulate walking/driving round an environment, turning left or right at junctions, which he trademarked as Virtual Travel® (VT). We discussed the possible ways to make a version of Cluedo on a computer, which would give, as much as possible, the same experience to the players as they obtained from the board game.

We decided that it would be possible to film a stately home with all the required rooms, such as a Drawing Room, Billiards Room, Conservatory, etc., using the VT technique he had developed. This involved taking an image every foot or so as the camera was moved forward and halted for the picture, and then when it got to a point where the user might want to go left or right, to take a 360° panorama so that the user could take another direction. We hooked up a broadcast-quality video camera mounted on a tripod trolley to an Apple Mac on a following trolley so that the image appeared immediately on the Mac's screen and so could be checked for accuracy of position and quality.

This worked perfectly, but in order to preserve continuity, we had to allow the house to be open to the public during the day and to avoid splashes of light from the windows we filmed in the evening and into the night. This meant that we had to light each of the rooms with large and hot film lights, which was really difficult as it would spoil the illusion if these special lights were seen in the shot. You can imagine how difficult it was to hide them when the camera was doing several 360° sweeps in each room. We were lucky in that Rickie Gauld, a great friend and wonderful ex-BBC lighting cameraman, was in charge of the camera and lights and, as always, did a superb job.

The most difficult rooms, which we left until last, were the Hall, staircase and upstairs landing. These had to be filmed in one session as otherwise, the re-placing of the lights would create discontinuities, and we had been told that the butler had to be around while we were filming to keep an eye on us. He normally retired at midnight, but we were less than half done by then, so we plied him with whisky until we finished shortly before daybreak. Apparently, he took several days to recover, which was not popular – but we had finished filming by then.

The house we filmed in was Holker Hall in Cumbria, owned by Lord and Lady Cavendish, which had all the necessary rooms and was laid out in the 1870s in such a way that almost all the rooms were interconnected with more than one door leading into another room, which would make the progress round them much more interesting for the game player.

We then constructed a virtual tour of the house with (virtual) clues hidden under, over and inside the furniture, such as wardrobes, chairs, tables and sofas. The distribution of clues was randomised and therefore different for each game so that there were many thousands of possible clue combinations meaning that it was impossible that – unlike the board game – a player would ever play the same game twice. In keeping with the realism of using an actual house, we used photographic images of real objects, such as train tickets, matchboxes, etc., for the clues, and video sequences of the characters such as Colonel Mustard, Miss Scarlet and so on.

These were matched to recorded voice-overs of the characters coming into view and responding to being questioned (by being clicked on), saying, for example, "I was never in the Library." Players could also click on a radio to hear a snatch of music or a newscast that might (or might not) offer a clue. The basis of the game, as in real life, was that the murderer was the only person with the victim in the murder room at the time of the murder, with the murder weapon. There was also a clever but simple secret information code process so that only the player taking his or her turn could be aware of the right answer to a question; nevertheless, all the other players had to pay attention and note down what happened during other players' turns, if they wanted to keep up and win the game.

The result was a much more deductive and entertaining game than the board game, with extraordinary variety and many amusing elements to be discovered as the game progressed. It .was undoubtedly one of the first true multimedia games and still one of the very few to feature real images. There have been many versions of Cluedo on computers since then, but none of them have approached the depth, realism, humour and variety of Foul Play, as it was eventually called (because Hasbro wanted to retain the Cluedo name).

It took about a year to create the game from scratch and was enormous fun to do, particularly the script-writing, filming and voice-over recording. We managed to insert many jokes into the script, playing on the eccentricities of the aristocracy, with much of it based on real incidents. For example, an officer in my regiment had built a complete suit of armour out of some redundant (I hope) steel filing cabinets and then sold it for a lot of money at an auction. We had one of the characters say, "I hear that Mr Boddy (the murder victim) is selling an old suit of armour made from filing cabinets. I'll definitely be making a bid, especially if he's wearing it!"

The game also featured secret passages – if you unwittingly clicked on a certain doorway, wardrobe or curtain, you were suddenly whisked off into another room at the other end of the house, which you might or might not want. The game had ten levels of difficulty but was designed so that after an hour, a telephone would ring, and when you clicked on it to pick it up, the Sergeant at the police station would give you a significant clue, e.g. "Our investigations have discovered that the murderer is a man". This ensured that a game did not go on for hours and hours and frustrate the players.

One of the principles that we learnt from the guys at Parker Bros/Hasbro who were helping us was that there should be no 'silver bullet' that would give an easy solution of the mystery, and in fact, there were always several routes to the solution, some faster than others, depending on the clues found.

We made some efforts to get Foul Play tested in schools to see whether teaching deductive reasoning would be a worthwhile benefit to children, but the very idea of a murder game – even though we made it clear there was no murder, body or blood shown in the game – was anathema to the teaching profession. Heaven forbid that children should be taught to think – they are at school to study the National Curriculum, not get an education that might actually fit them for the world outside, and as for teaching them to deduce, i.e. to think, what might that lead to?

Military Mission – In Step At Last

William Donelson and I had founded The Armchair Travel Company to produce and market Foul Play, and a year or two later, we were asked to produce a CD-ROM version of a virtual tour of a Royal Navy Type-42 Destroyer that William had made first on videodisc and later on a specialist DVI system that never made the commercial grade. The idea was to install it in specially-equipped trucks that the Royal Navy sent round the country on recruiting drives and at the annual Royal Tournament exhibition at Earls Court.

It is notoriously difficult to control a large group of school children in the potentially dangerous environment found on the decks of a Destroyer or other naval vessels, as they can fall overboard, trip at bulkheads, fall down companionways and so on. Also, many of the compartments are quite small, so very few of the children can be in one at a time or hear the commentary from a guide as to what it is used for. Also, a visit hardly gives the feeling of a ship at sea with engines, radar, machinery in operation and guns firing.

The Royal Navy, therefore, commissioned us to produce a new, up-to-date version of the virtual tour and to film it on HMS Exeter, which we did during an exercise with the Dutch Navy in 2005. The film crew shot 130 panoramas over several days, including all the decks, engine rooms, bridge, mess decks and all the passages and companionways in both directions so that the user could 'walk' around the ship with almost complete freedom. He/She could enter one of the many compartments, look around, click on over 4,000 items of equipment, see the Sea Dart missile launched, the 4.5-inch gun and machine guns fired and get explanations of how they worked.

He could also click on many members of the crew, seen during the virtual tour and see a video of them explaining what their tasks were. We asked for humorous reminiscences, and one of the cooks told us that he had been cooking jacket potatoes for the entire crew (250) and had told a new recruit to the galley to "stick a fork in each potato before you put them in the oven". Sometime later, he was looking for forks to lay out and couldn't find any. He suddenly realised what he had said, looked in the ovens and found 250 forks bent out of shape with the heat, sticking in the potatoes.

There is also a database enabling the user to click on an item of equipment, such as fire extinguishers and see where they were all located. This is by far the largest and most comprehensive virtual tour ever produced on CD-ROM and was a huge success for the Navy, so much so that they ordered about 35,000 disc copies to go to every school in the country, as well as using the disc for many years for recruiting purposes. We even heard that officers transferring to a Type-42 Destroyer used it to familiarise themselves with the ship before joining it. It was also used at the Operator

Mechanic Training School at Gosport. We even got a wonderful write-up of the system in "Dust or Magic; Secrets of Successful Multimedia Design", Bob Hughes's definitive study of multimedia, in which he described William and myself, uniquely, as "heroes of the multimedia revolution".

This extraordinary project led to a series of programmes for the military, starting with one for the Royal Armoured Corps, giving a virtual tour of a Challenger 2 tank, which we filmed at RAC Bovington in Dorset, a familiar location from my Young Officer's Course in the Army, learning all about tanks. We were shown around by the archetype of the quietly competent professional soldier, Corporal-Major Mike Jenkins of the Life Guards.

Tall, spare and with a wry smile, he was everything that you could want and looked after us magnificently. It was not easy filming inside the Challenger, which had by then only just been introduced to the Army and was being put through its paces on the test tracks and ranges at Bovington, because space in the turret was very limited, and so the panoramic camera had to be carefully positioned and set up, and then we had to scramble out of shot, before triggering the exposure.

We had to doctor the images taken in the tank so that curious eyes could not gauge the thickness of the armour on the top of the turret nor guess the depth of penetration of the projectiles by examining their length.

The tank had the new 120mm gun with a separate charge and projectile. I asked what the maximum range was and was told that they had fired a high-velocity armoured-piercing test round on maximum elevation of the gun, and it was later picked up on a beach in Northern France and returned to them; hmmm. I told Mike of a similar incident from my days at Bovington when the officer running the gunnery course, Richard Cliff, became so fed up with a fishing boat slowly crossing and re-crossing the danger area (from which it was prohibited) in the bay beyond the ranges that he ordered me to fire, at maximum elevation, a round with a warhead containing sand.

He said to put it in the trawler's general direction, but I took him a bit literally, and the shot landed about 20 yards astern of the fishing boat, which then sped off out of sight. Wiping his brow, Richard said, "Well, Beckett, that was nearly the end of your military career – and mine!" He got his own back on me by ordering me to go quickly up a steep slope on the tank driving course, over the ridge at the top and down the other side. What he hadn't told me was that at the bottom of the almost sheer downward slope was a small lake, so I had no choice but to enter it at about 15 miles an hour, as it is impossible to halt a 55-ton tank on a steep incline.

About two hundred gallons of muddy water entered the tank through the open driver's hatch in which I was sitting, almost drowning me. The only satisfying element was that when we had to drain the tank that evening, I persuaded a very tiresome young officer called Tony Emerson (who had not seen the incident) to crawl under the tank and unscrew the drainage plate, with results that were predictable to everyone but him.

The CD-ROM programme was a great success, and like the Navy programme, was used at the Royal Tournament and sent round the Army's recruiting offices, with the exception of my regiment's own office in Leicester, where the officer in charge was so technically backward that he refused to put it to work, even though a number of our particular cavalry regiment's officers and NCOs featured in it – you can lead a horse(man) to water, but you can't make him think.

The Virtual Tank discs led to a very profitable series of deals with BAe Systems for programmes used by their marketing people. In succession we filmed their Braveheart (AS90) 155mm howitzer, issued to the British Army, which was akin to a tank but with a powerful gun firing shells up to 30 miles with incredible accuracy (and of which some 30 have been sent to Ukraine), the 105mm Light Gun which was used in the Falklands, Iraq and Afghanistan, BAe's armoured mortar carrying vehicle, and most notably, the 155mm air transportable howitzer, made from titanium, which was bought by the US and Canadian Armies.

Making programmes on all these vehicles and guns was an extraordinary set of experiences as we filmed them in the open and on the ranges as well as on giant turntables in their hangar at Barrow-on-Furness so that the gun could be turned round in a series of small steps, with an image captured at each step. This allowed the playback to show the gun being turned round through 360˙ on screen whilst it was elevated and depressed. The presenter could then point out its various features as it went around, many of which, when clicked on, had short video/audio/graphics elements.

With each programme, there were also a number of videos showing the equipment in use in various roles or options that showed how it could be used, together with other elements, such as the types of ammunition. The point was that taking this programme to the user, even when the cost of making it was included, was much cheaper and more convenient than moving a gun to the potential customer's location. We made numerous versions of each programme as the guns were modified and upgraded, and applied different language options.

The programmes were also designed to run automatically at exhibitions such as the biennial DSEi, though they could be immediately interrupted and used interactively by someone clicking the mouse/trackball and choosing one of the aspects of the programme, which were all visible on the home screen. Mike Jenkins was invaluable in helping us with the making of the programmes, setting up the lights, moving the vehicle or gun around, and all with a smile and a joke which kept us going when things got tough, as we ran up against deadlines.

BAe Systems appreciated, above all, the realism of the images, which showed off the guns and armoured vehicles and which, being interactive, were so much more use than a video. The presenter could remain in control of his subject matter by choosing which elements he showed, thus tailoring his presentation specifically to his audience. The film was taken at high resolution so that when the programme was displayed on a large projection screen, the images were crystal clear in high definition, and all this from an ordinary laptop which the marketing people carried around everywhere with them anyway.

The virtual travel technique clearly worked best on ships and armoured vehicles and guns, as opposed to aircraft, and was feasible only when the ship or vehicle had already been built, as opposed to Computer Graphics Images (CGI), which could be used to produce and display 3-D models of as yet unbuilt equipment – though CGI on its own is really more single- than multi-media.

We also made a number of programmes for Alvis Vehicles, the main one being on the Scarab reconnaissance and command vehicle already mentioned. I managed to get these programmes underway because, after trying for many months to get a meeting with Alvis in their London head office, finally, in frustration, I wrote to the appropriately named Richard Wigley, their Business Development Director, saying *"As you may be aware, I have been trying to contact you since early February, and I must say that in thirty years in business, you have been the hardest person to contact that I have ever encountered, beating a personal best, recorded some years ago, of 55 telephone calls, letters etc. If I may say so, you have proved as elusive as one of your company's excellent recce vehicles in the hands of a skilled commander!"*

It worked; he fixed up a meeting through his assistant Mary-Ann Griffiths, and we had a great relationship with all their people until they were sold to Vickers several years later.

The ultimate filming moment for the military was the shoot we did on HMS Vanguard, one of the Trident missile submarines based at Faslane. We had been invited to film a compartment of the nuclear submarine while it was in dock so that the environment we created could be used in their dockside training school, where the only visual materials they previously had were some blueprints of the sub, which, because of all the detail, were incredibly difficult to follow. We were met by Lt. Cmdrs. Jim Hammersley and John Warden at Glasgow Airport and took a hire car round Loch Lomond to Faslane.

The weather was terrible with driving rain and we had, in fact, to take the High Road round the Loch as the Low Road was flooded. Nearing Faslane, we came over the crest of a mountain and, in the gathering darkness under heavily overcast, almost black skies, were presented with the sight of the naval base and dock below us. Lying menacingly in the water was *HMS Vanguard*, the epitome of Cold War menace – Len Deighton would have felt quite at home here.

Needless to say, the dockside was guarded by a number of large men in black jumpsuits with helmets and visors and carrying submachine guns. We entered the dock through heavy top-to-toe turnstiles, having been identified with the help of our guides Hammersley and Warden, and clambered down into the vast submarine.

William had not opted for the standard plastic helmet and consequently banged his head a number of times on the numerous projections, such as valves, that the working compartments are full of. Being a bit taller, I had taken the wiser course, and William told me later that he could check on my progress and location by the succession of thuds as my helmet hit those projections. We carefully filmed the Forward Escape Compartment, which, for obvious reasons, every crew member is trained on, and were then invited to the Wardroom to meet some of the crew.

Passing through the Control compartment and then past the huge enclosed tubes which held the missiles, we finally arrived at the Wardroom, which was just as large as that in a Destroyer, and were greeted by the Captain and some of his officers, all of whom were incredibly friendly and full of jokes and laughter - obviously the créme de la créme of the Royal Navy.

After a dram or two, we retired and left them to get on with the serious business of providing our nuclear deterrent. I felt we were in good hands; whatever the Government chose to do, I would definitely have trusted these men with our future.

Infuriatingly, the division of BAe Systems that supplied and maintained the Trident submarines scotched the deal for us to film the entire submarine in spite of the fact that the Training School at Faslane tested our programme on the next group of inductees and achieved results that were as good as taking the trainees on a tour of the boat. In other words, there was no discernible difference in knowledge levels between a group trained on our system and one taken on board and instructed there – as and when a submarine was available.

Clearly, it was much cheaper, more convenient and just as effective to use our virtual tour as to use a real one. In this competitive environment, BAe was aided by an organisation called HVR, which had a photogrammetry system that could, with some effort, create an accurate CGI environment and, presented with two choices – us or HVR – the MoD took the third option, which was to do nothing. Obviously, they felt it was not really necessary to use the best and most-cost effective methods to train our nuclear submariners about such vital issues as using the escape system properly. To hell with Health & Safety, this is the MoD, and we know what's best for you.

In any event, a year or two later, HVR were a tremendous help to us in recommending our services to the Historic Dockyard, Chatham, which was faced with the problem of how to enable disabled visitors to clamber round the WWII Destroyer, *HMS Cavalier*, and even more so, the Cold War diesel electric Submarine, *HMs/m Ocelot*, whose circular bulkhead doors require visitors to scramble through head first or swing through feet first.

Cavalier was undergoing a major programme of repair, helped by the Lottery Fund, and quite large areas were not really in a condition to be visited because it had been shamefully neglected whilst moored on Tyneside as an attraction. *Ocelot*, in contrast, was obviously a much newer ship, having been built in the 1960s, as opposed to the 1940s with *Cavalier*, and so was in relatively pristine condition when transferred to Chatham. We filmed these ships over a number of days down at Chatham using lights to brighten the numerous dark corners, not least the engine and boiler rooms. The ex-Royal Navy volunteers and maintenance workers were amazingly helpful as they rapidly caught on to the reality that, for us, it was as much a matter of a task of love as of money.

We were determined, as always, to make the ships look as good and as interesting as possible, and I even went through the archives of the Imperial War Museum to find as much visual information as I could about WWII destroyers and 'O'-class submarines. I also unearthed some video programmes made by the BBC, called the "*Perisher*" series, about the training and testing of potential captains, when the candidate was invited to test his skills in avoiding, or sinking, a destroyer hunting his sub.

Obviously, no real depth charges or torpedoes were used, but for the candidates having to do the mental arithmetic to work out in real-time the angles, depth to run at, distance to the destroyer and then issue the appropriate commands under pressure, it was all too real. The excellent footage was complemented by some taken on the North Atlantic convoys featuring a Royal Canadian Navy corvette and of a race off the Firth of Forth between *Cavalier* and another destroyer in the early 1970s. It is exhilarating stuff, and I believe that many of the disabled, as well as those of the able who use it, enjoy the programmes as much as an actual visit.

Two copies of the CD-ROM programme are run on PCs installed in a concrete shed on the dockside at Chatham, and we upgraded the programmes a few years later to take advantage of bigger screens, faster processors and new footage of a number of re-furbished compartments in Cavalier. We also included a smaller programme on *HMS Gannet*, which was one of the original sail/steam gunboats policing the Empire in the late Victorian and pre-WWI era. She has been magnificently restored, and a visit to her is now very rewarding, as it is to the other ships. We dug out some wonderful historic pictures of her also and provided animations of the "Up Funnel, Down Screw" or "Down Funnel, Up Screw" sequences which converted her quickly from a sailing ship to a steam-powered vessel or vice versa, when either the weather or tactical situation demanded it and the funnel and screw needed to be retracted or extended. Not surprisingly, that command passed into music hall history.

In all, it was a delight to deal with Richard Holdsworth, the CEO of the Historic Dockyard, who exemplifies the best type of manager – highly knowledgeable, always enthusiastic and prepared to lend a hand to whatever was going on. I understand he has transformed the finances, operation and popularity of the Dockyard, which is, to say the least, somewhat off the normal tourist track but is now a world-class heritage site.

Another project that began originally for the RAC wound up at the Firepower Museum at nearby Woolwich. Essentially, it started as a virtual terrain project to train tank commanders in the crucial task of selecting optimum fire positions. Unfortunately, the then Director of the RAC, the late Major-General James Short, was completely uninterested in the project, and it died temporarily until we resuscitated it as an artillery game which we built for BAe Systems, sponsors of the Firepower Museum, which displayed all things connected with the artillery.

Basically, the idea was to simulate the hitting of a variety of targets with the appropriate shells fired from a 105mm Light Gun in a number of locations on Salisbury Plain and thereby qualify as a master gunner – or not. We had filmed about 30 panoramas on the Plain, together with a number of sequences of the gun being loaded, aimed and fired, and these proved to make a very playable game with the realism engendered by the real panoramic images and video sequences and actual range tables.

This was the only exhibit at the Museum to exhibit the realities of laying and firing an artillery piece at a target, and we intended to develop it further to make it into an artillery duel with another gun, manned by another visitor at another PC firing back at you, the object being to destroy it before it destroyed you. The connection would have been made over the Internet so that it could become a distance-independent game.

Needless to say, the head Gunner at Woolwich made it as difficult as possible for us to implement and install it, as his feathers were ruffled because he had not thought of it first. It replaced a very bad and completely trivial game that did not work at all and on which a fortune had apparently been expended. You can guess whose idea that was. Our game was then due to be installed and run at Fort Nelson near Portsmouth, which also had a variety of guns of all shapes and sizes, but, if you can believe it, someone had 'borrowed' the camouflage tent in which it was due to be placed and the people there were afraid to ask for the tent back, having spent far more than the value of the tent in equipment etc. to run the game. After several visits there to try to get the show on the road, it began to appear that the more help I gave them, the further away the date of implementation receded. Finally, I gave up and left them to their squabbles.

Virtual Travel – Did You Really Want To Go There?

As a result of the development and publishing of the Foul Play game, I was in a good position in 1995 to approach the division of the giant publishers, Bertelsmann, which had an offshoot called Bertelsmann Media Group or BMG, with the idea of creating a series of virtual tours of top heritage sites.

Fortunately, there was a guy there, Ian Matthias, who I knew quite well from when we were both at Virgin. He came into our office in London SW6 and, after talking to me and William Donelson, told us that he thought the combination would work well because William D was obviously well able to do the technical work, and I should be able, through my contacts, to set up deals with the heritage sites, which were, as it turned out, often run by retired generals or admirals. BMG had recently published a CD-ROM disc on the Louvre, which had been very well received and gave a fairly detailed presentation of the building's history, together with an overall view of its major exhibits.

Negotiating the contract with BMG was a nightmare, and at one point, I was at loggerheads with our lawyer and William D, who both felt I was being unreasonable in standing out for a particular clause which had to do with termination. I refused to give in on it, which, as we shall see later on, was extremely fortunate.

Then BMG wanted us to demonstrate our technology running on a PC – our software only ran, at that point, on Apple Macs and they were refusing to sign the contract until they saw it on a PC. Again, I refused to give in, and they finally signed just before our deadline, which had much to do with the dates I was going on holiday.

After this rather fraught start, things got underway in the autumn of 1996, but I had already been in touch with the then Black Rod at the Houses of Parliament – General Sir Edward Jones, a tall, dark-haired and very impressive man who was a terrific help in getting the project approved, not only by the Lords, but also by the Commons, in the shape of the Serjeant-at-Arms, and steering the project through the various committees of both houses.

General Edward was the most effective military man I have ever had to deal with, and I quickly came to understand why he had made full four-star General, and though he was a very entertaining and amusing chap, if he thought we were falling down on our commitments or responsibilities, he made it very clear that he was not going to tolerate any messing about. Sadly, he died comparatively young some years ago, having retired after being Black Rod for five or six years. A mutual friend told me that his daughter, who was the General's goddaughter, and the General used to stand on their heads whenever they met each other!

In fact, we had to begin filming before the contract was signed with Parliament because we had agreed to film in the Summer

Recess when neither House was sitting. The actual filming had to take place in the early morning before tourists and others invaded the palace, when the only people about were the cleaners, who were, I believe, mostly from the Philippines.

How that squared with the intense security there, I am not sure, and I never felt the urge to ask, but it frequently gave us a problem because it was very hard to make them understand that we needed them out of sight, as they were always walking into shot at the critical moment. The filming technique we used was unusual, to say the least, because basically, there were two elements to it: the panorama shots and the film of the connecting walkways between the panorama points.

In 1996, there were no digital cameras, so we used film throughout. And for the panoramas, we took twelve shots in a circle with an SLR camera and the results were then processed, scanned, digitised and put through a process that allowed the images to be joined seamlessly to produce a QuickTime panorama. We used a wide-angle lens set up in portrait mode so that most of the ceiling could also be in shot except that part directly overhead. Standard films were 36 exposures, so, with luck we got three panoramas on each film – except when a Philippino cleaner came suddenly into view.

We wanted to interconnect the panorama points by film in order to give the illusion of walking through the Palace, so we used a 16 mm movie camera in manual single-shot mode, as the 36-shot maximum of an SLR, before reloading, had far too few images. This camera was mounted on a wheelchair in which the cameraman, Rickie Gauld, sat whilst I wheeled him forward from one panorama point to the next, stopping every foot or so to take another shot.

We then had to do the journey back between each panorama point so that users could walk around the Palace in both directions. You might think that video was the obvious answer, but we had tried that, and if there was anything but a blank wall on either side of the room, which never happened at the Palace, the user saw so much high-frequency shimmer or moiré effect that the images were impossible to use. We also put the walkway images through a process that stabilised each image relative to its neighbours and another that colour-balanced them to match the panoramas.

We used a similar filming technique for the Type-42 virtual tour, but in hand-held mode there without the wheelchair, so that the images were rather more jerky, which was acceptable in a military product. We also filmed panoramas from the top of the massive Victoria Tower, which was, when it was completed in 1860 to house Parliament's records, the tallest square tower in the world, situated at the opposite end of the Palace to Big Ben, and obviously, we had to do the Clock Tower, as well as a number of external panoramas on the Terrace by the river and at various other points round the outside. Fortunately there was at that time no scaffolding on the Palace.

After the filming was complete, which took a week, William D and his team were then faced with the task of sorting and collating the many thousands of frames, processing them and making them into a completely connected virtual tour of the Palace. When we had finished this we showed it to BMG, who were completely bowled over by it.

Photo-realistic virtual reality had arrived because it was the first time that, on a computer, people could move smoothly through a real photographic environment, choosing from a number of available routes, panning around and looking up and down to see what was there. And in the Palace of Westminster there is plenty there to see – you don't stick around for almost a thousand years without accumulating some points of interest.

Those points of interest meant that we had to allow the user to click on anything of interest that they could see, and for this, we took still photographs of all the objects in view, from the wallpaper to statues, furniture, paintings, murals – some of them 40 feet long – and so on. Stephen Davies and I then wrote a script describing all of them and also a general commentary for each panorama, which he recorded, and we then digitised and incorporated into the programme. There were no less than 450 mini-movies describing the objects and some 90 or so panoramas.

We also included music deemed appropriate for each panorama and inter-connecting walkways, such as the Minute Waltz for the Clock Tower and Handel's Water Music for the Terrace. This gave a continuity and smoothness to the programme and set the scene for each room. I was very gratified when a music aficionado from IBM, for whom we later made another programme, singled out the music for special praise.

William had terrible problems making the mini-movies appear on the screen in front of the panoramas so that the user could revert immediately to the panorama that he was in when the playback of the mini-movie was completed. Macromedia Director, which we were using for the main programming, fought for supremacy with Apple's QuickTime, which we were using for the panoramas, and it took William months to resolve this crucial issue.

We decided that we might as well make the Explore Parliament programme, as it was called, a tour-de-force, however long it took, rather than skimping on the content in any way, and that was borne out by the success that the programme achieved in schools – in competition with a very 'thin' and third-rate programme made by the BBC, whose production was paid for by the taxpayer, who then had to stump up a further £10 for each copy sold to schools – iniquitous. Where in the BBC's Charter does it say that they are permitted to spend taxpayers' money developing programmes that cannot be shown on television and which compete in the market for

CD-ROM products with those developed by the private sector, at private expense; and then sell them at a profit?

Not surprisingly, the BBC can afford to undercut programmes developed by the private sector and use their broadcast education programmes to promote and market their CD-ROMs. I believe it is true to say that the BBC hardly produced a single educational CD-ROM of note or of lasting benefit and quality. Most of their programmes feature two-dimensional cartoon characters. It is not as if the BBC does such a great job any longer in the broadcast TV field. Most of its output now is cheap TV – reality shows, cookery, property, gardening and quiz shows, and frequently, the main objective is to humiliate some, or preferably most, of the participants.

To cap it all, Parliament itself, who should have known better, called their website, developed with funding from Research Machines – Explore Parliament. We objected, naturally, but they went ahead anyway after writing us a very discourteous and rather nasty letter. Interestingly, our programme filled an entire CD-ROM and took approximately 10 hours to play every movie and visit every panorama – almost exactly the same duration as a series of ten one-hour BBC TV programmes made some eight or nine years before. It was just that our programme contained about ten times as much content but at one-quarter of the cost.

In parallel with the development of Explore Parliament, we filmed St. Paul's Cathedral and Westminster Abbey, which were both also run administratively by ex-military men, the first of which became a major saga because of the necessity of filming it all at one time and at night. This was because we could not close it during the day due to all the tourists and the services planned months ahead. Obviously, at night – it was December – we had to light the cathedral, which we did with powerful tungsten lamps powered by a generator in a lorry parked by the North Transept.

We also decided to remove all the rather unsightly brown chairs which cluttered up the nave and the Great Circle under the dome and thereby expose the wonderful chequered marble floor. This was a major performance because there were more than 3,500 chairs, and it took us several hours to park them all on their trolleys and move them outside the West Door. We then had to sweep the floor as there were many piles of dust. Whilst this was going on the lighting crew set up the lights, and William and Rickie got them adjusted so that they were not in shot from any of the angles that we were due to film from.

We had persuaded the Cathedral authorities to turn on all the outside lights and this had the unexpected bonus that the windows appeared on film to be blue, as by Sir Christopher Wren's dictum, they contained little stained glass, except at the East End. By midnight we had all the chairs cleared, and the lights set up and turned on, so we sat down on the marble floor and ate our dinner, which was a Chinese meal taken away from Mr Poons in Soho – delicious!

While we were doing this, a mouse scurried right across the floor of the Great Circle and down the stairs to the crypt. Sadly, we were the only people to see the amazing sight of the vast cathedral, beautifully lit, totally empty of clutter, with the beautiful marble floor completely visible and in complete silence – unforgettable.

The filming, which we did in a similar fashion to Parliament but with the 36mm film camera on a tripod trolley this time, took the rest of the night, finishing at about 6 am, and I then had to rush the film to be processed at Technicolor near Heathrow, so we could see the results asap. We replaced the chairs the next day and filmed the crypt the following night. All seemed OK until we checked the content of the film and suddenly realised that Technicolor had thrown away the first few frames and last few frames of each film taken by the panorama SLR camera. Though this is normal practice in film processing, where every cameraman shoots a foot or two of film before and after the real shooting, in this case, it left us with panoramas that were several frames and thus many degrees short of the full 360°.

So, gritting our teeth and claiming from our production insurance, we determined to repeat the process the following February. Fortunately, St. Paul's were very cooperative, and we repeated the filming, but with a proper panoramic film camera that we had acquired in the meantime. This used 220 format film of 65mm width and shot an entire panorama with one exposure, using a slit-scan technique with the film passing the slit as the head rotated 400°, with the bonus that we could shoot 12 or 13 panoramas on one film.

This time, after we had removed the chairs outside the West Door, we found that Princess Michael of Kent had arranged a photo shoot outside the West Door on the evening of the next day after the shoot, while we had arranged to leave the chairs there for a day in case we had to re-shoot for any reason. The upshot was that, at her insistence, all 3,500 chairs had to be moved inside again and then out again when she had finished, even though her photo shoot could easily have been re-arranged. They don't call her Princess Pushy for nothing.

Apart from that hassle, everything went right this time, although we were rather surprised that none of the staff – apart from two electricians on duty, of which more later – bothered to take up our invitation to see the Cathedral as Wren had intended. We discovered that we took much less time and with far fewer people to set up unobtrusive lights covering the entire Cathedral than the BBC did just to cover the Nave for some State occasion.

In fact, we could not use any of the sodium vapour lights permanently installed at the Cathedral because they threw a ghastly orange hue like a motorway service station, though they have now been completely replaced with excellent lighting and the whole Cathedral has been cleaned, gilded where appropriate and tidied up inside and out at a cost of £40 million, in contrast to the mess we found there. In fact we had to process the images very carefully to make the then stained and dirty stonework look as good as possible.

One new feature that is definitely not an improvement, at least from the aesthetic viewpoint, is the superfluous addition of a polished wooden dais on the floor of the Great Circle near the Quire. No doubt intended to bring the clergy closer to the congregation or some such clerical baloney, it wrecks the beautiful symmetric effect of the black and white marble tiled floor. If Wren had thought something like that was needed, he would have designed the cathedral differently.

In fact, we also filmed, both inside and out, the Great Model, now housed in an inaccessible but lovely room in the Triforium above the Nave. The Great Model was Wren's earlier and preferred design and took the form of a Greek Cross. It would have answered, beautifully, the perceived problem dealt with by the dais, but the clergy at the time insisted on a Latin Cross with a nice long Nave so that they could progress along it and be seen – if not admired – by the congregation.

Whilst we were making the programme, I arranged to meet Martin Stancliffe, the then architect looking after St. Paul's, whose father, curiously, had married Virginia and I at St. Margaret's, Parliament Square, many years before. He showed us round the spaces above the dome and took us to see the circular chain that Wren had had installed to withstand the outward spreading pressure caused by the 50,000-ton weight of the Dome.

He also told us about the stainless steel beams that were inserted into the interior of the main pillars in the late 1920s when it was discovered that, as a result of drainage ditches being dug near the West end of the Cathedral, cracks had appeared and the cathedral was closed under a dangerous structure order. He also showed us the flying buttresses, so necessary to contain the outward pressures on the walls caused by the heavy roof of the Nave and Quire, but hidden by the curtain walls, so the Cathedral, unlike Westminster Abbey, for example, looks so homogenous from the outside. A fascinating, and for a layman, unique tour.

We also visited the bell tower, with its Great Tom hour bell and quarter bells driven by the clock designed by my great-great uncle, Edmund Beckett-Denison.

"Just think, my dearest, if this is what man is capable of in the 17th century, imagine what he will be capable of by the 20th!!!"

Later that Spring, we determined to film Westminster Abbey, with whose management, like St. Paul's and the Houses of Parliament, we had signed a contract. This presented a different problem in that the Abbey is really a series of differently sized rooms, each built at different periods and with an incredible clutter of statues, tombs and memorials of every conceivable type, making it, in effect, the nation's attic, containing dusty and often forgotten statues or obscure relics of nearly a thousand years of English history.

There are lots of side chapels off the side aisles, all lit differently and with varying amounts of outside light coming through the stained glass windows. Our team performed a miracle of photo processing so that we were able to produce a nicely colour-balanced virtual tour, allowing the visitor to move round the entire Abbey in both directions and to visit all the side chapels, etc.

The high-level physical tour that Christian Smithers, our photographer and picture-processing man, and I took around the upper levels of the Abbey was equally fascinating but completely different to that at St. Paul's. We were guided about the upper regions by the appropriately named Mr Buttress, the man in charge of the actual building, and part of it involved edging along a narrow walkway around the North Transept with a 150 ft drop below us and holding – for dear life – onto a narrow steel cable of the type used on a yacht to stop you going overboard – but we didn't have a harness to clip onto it. To make it feel more precarious, it was a very windy day. Not a moment for vertigo.

Anyway, Christian did manage to take some unique and beautiful photographs, as he also did inside the Abbey for the memorials, statues and slabs on the floor, a notable one being that of the 17th-century playwright Ben Jonson, who was buried vertically – with a consequently small slab, inscribed "O rare Ben Jonson". Who would not want an epitaph even half as good? Even Nelson was beguiled by the Abbey, as he was reported to have shouted "Westminster Abbey! or Glorious Victory" as he boarded the 112-gun Sant Nicolas, and then from it boarded and captured the 80-gun San Josep at the Battle of Cape St. Vincent. Ironically, but appropriately, he was buried in St. Paul's.

These productions gave me and everyone at Armchair Travel, the little company we had created to make these programmes, an unparalleled experience and view of perhaps the three most interesting and historic buildings in England. In fact, the work had only really just started as we had to create mini-movies of the sites, and we were well into this when I was asked to attend a meeting at St. Paul's.

The background to this was that we had agreed to pay the costs of the previously mentioned electricians – who had actually just sat in their own workshop and returned to their homes at some time in the night without bothering to tell us. We were only in the Cathedral until midnight the following day and, so their total overtime was a maximum of 18 hours each. I was stunned, therefore, to receive a bill from the Works Department of St. Paul's for over £8,400.

This included the costs of seven or eight people for four or five nights plus a team of extra people during the day for several days. Naturally, I objected to this and was, in due course, summoned to the Chapter House adjoining the Cathedral to discuss it. The meeting was chaired by George Cassidy, later the Bishop of Southwell, who was then Archdeacon and Canon at St. Paul's. I found, to my surprise, that Canon Middleton from Westminster Abbey was also at the meeting.

A very unpleasant man called, I believe, Stones (in charge of building works) weighed into me from St. Paul's, making all sorts of wild accusations backed up by Middleton. I defended myself as best I could, and after what felt like hours, Cassidy asked me if I had anything further had say in my defence.

As the clock of St. Paul's was striking at that moment I asked whether they knew the name of the person who had designed the clock that had caused it to strike. Someone replied Lord Grimthorpe, so I retorted, "Yes, Edmund Beckett-Denison, my great-great uncle. It was he who designed it and he did it for free. I think you are showing a lack of charity over the present issue in which you are proposing to prevent us from producing a unique product, at no cost to yourselves, but that you will be able to sell in the Cathedral shop for a handsome profit".

There was no answer to this, but I did savour the moment that I was able, justly, to accuse senior representatives of the Church of England of a lack of charity – which we are told by Our Lord was the greatest of the three cardinal virtues (Faith and Hope being the others).

There was a considerable aftermath to this meeting in that I received a very nasty letter from Charles Russell, lawyers to both St. Paul's and Westminster Abbey, saying that we could not continue with either of the programmes. However, I found an excellent lawyer called Mark Dautlich at Olswang, the specialist media lawyers, who replied with such a brilliant response that they both had to give in.

At about the same time as we were making the programme at St. Paul's, a Channel Four team had been given permission to make a fly-on-the-wall TV programme on the working life of the Cathedral. It duly came out in three one-hour documentaries which were highly critical of the operation of, amongst others, the works and accounting departments, implying they were ripping off the Cathedral's funds and confirmed it by showing a meeting at which it was apparent that the Works Department (under the a/m Stones) was not remotely under the control of the Registrar, the senior executive of the Cathedral. I also found out from an article in Private

Eye that Canon Middleton had received £45,000 from the Abbey's funds to buy himself a cottage in the country – charity certainly worked for him, even if he did not work for it.

And they had the nerve to condemn me for making documentary programmes on these national monuments, at almost no cost to them, and which would be sold in their shops, bringing them considerable revenue.

At about this time, we received, out of the blue, a letter from BMG saying that they were terminating our contract without even giving a reason. I immediately called in Mark Dautlich, and he confirmed that BMG could not break the contract without our agreement – exactly the clause that I had insisted on including when we negotiated the deal. There were some rather protracted discussions, and then we met up with BMG's lawyers at Olswang's offices for the crunch meeting.

BMG immediately conceded that they had broken the contract, and then it was just a matter of agreeing to the compensation and terms. We walked away with the rights to all the material that we had created, plus £40 grand and BMG had to pay Olswang's costs. Bearing in mind that, at the time, Bertelsmann, BMG's owners, were the largest publishers in Europe and one of the largest in the world, we reckoned we had not done too badly.

Actually, the people we had met at BMG were really very nice and helpful, and the decision had been forced on them by an edict from above that BMG was being moved to California to concentrate on the Computer Games market. When we had discussed audio and music content with them for the St. Paul's project, in a moment of enthusiasm, I inadvertently suggested that we use "swelling organ music" as one virtually travelled into the Cathedral, which caused some hilarity amongst the girls from BMG.

As with Parliament, we created hundreds of mini-movies for St. Paul's and Westminster Abbey using the still photographs that Christian had taken in order to identify and describe all aspects of the interiors of the cathedral and abbey, especially the monuments, but also the architecture and history; an abbreviated version of the comprehensive timeline that we had created for Parliament. I showed them to the Registrar, who was a Brigadier, and he was happy with all of them except that he felt I had been unfair to General Freyberg.

The New Zealander was a VC, had several DSOs and was a friend of Churchill's, but as commander-in-chief of the island, he managed to lose Crete, having been informed where and when the German airborne invasion would take place from Enigma decrypts. He ignored them, concentrating on a potential seaborne invasion, so allowing the parachutists to take the main airfield, and consequently, he lost the island – one of the major British disasters of WWII. He also bore some responsibility for the protracted failure to take Monte

Cassino later on during the battle for Italy. Undoubtedly a very brave man, but he was perhaps not a great commander.

Having finished the St. Paul's project and produced a CD-ROM disc, as we had for Parliament, we had to go back to the Abbey and tell them that it was not really feasible to produce a disc for them because the market had changed and the Internet had rendered obsolete the market for discs. We offered to make an Internet version for them, but the proposal was turned down, so we decided instead to make a programme on the Taj Mahal; after all, which would you rather see, the most beautiful monument in the world or the Abbey – fine as it undoubtedly is?

This was a shame, but the cost of producing a comprehensive product on the Abbey would have been prohibitive, given the amount of content that was involved. The disc on St. Paul's sold quite well in their cathedral shop, thanks to a 'kiosk' system I installed there that showed visitors the programme and allowed them to interact with it.

Research told us that the Taj Mahal was one of the very few places that were known to almost everyone, or at any rate, those who would likely be surfing the net, so we brought in a couple of investors who helped us fund the project, specifically the expedition to do the filming. Luckily, my sister had married an Indian *Rajput,* and her elder daughter had developed a lot of family contacts in India, so with the help of those relations, we launched an assault on the bureaucracy of the Archaeological Survey of India, which controls and manages every important Indian archaeological site.

We were very lucky in that a remote relation of my niece, called Mala Tandan or familiarly Babli, ran a travel agency in Delhi specialising in helping film companies operate in India and was prepared to put in the effort required to get us permission to film there. Her staff were equally determined and helped organise a meeting for me with the charming and urbane Director of the Survey, who sadly was killed in a car crash a few years later.

I sat in his office while we talked, and he took various calls, and I noticed his male assistant come in and park an armful of brown manilla folders bound in red tape – yes, that's where the term comes from – on his desk! We talked, and the Director took more calls, and then before I left, the assistant re-emerged and took away all the folders. I realised that the method of operation was to be able to say, if questioned, that the files had been "shown" to the Director, even if he seldom, if ever, had the time to actually read them.

The Director's two main executives were the people we had to convince, and we had already managed to get one of them on our side before I left for India. However, that automatically meant that the other was dead set against the scheme, though he also had to sign it off. Fortunately Babli had an assistant who arranged for me to meet this fellow the afternoon before I had to fly to Agra to join the rest of the team to film on the following day.

We talked on and on for hours without getting a clear decision, and somewhat reluctantly, I left to catch the last plane, having been assured that Babli's man would get the Survey man to sign a fax that evening. This he eventually did, but in order to do so he had to sit in the fellow's office until he eventually capitulated at 9 pm that evening, and even had to agree to drive him home.

Babli called me to say everything was OK, but when I met the guy in charge of the monument in Agra the next morning, he refused to accept that we had permission despite the fax. However, I was able to do an end run around him because, by chance, I had the Director's home number and called him and asked him to override the local manager – which, fortunately, he did.

When we began filming, it was again nearly aborted because the local manager's deputy suddenly demanded 10 lakhs of rupees, about £10,000, and told us that filming was not possible as repairs to the roof were in progress. With the fax in hand and a threat to call the Director, by now a friend of mine, I managed to head them off and secured the help of the foreman who took us everywhere we needed to go, including the roof, which it turned out, just had a few scaffolding poles lying about that were easily moved out of shot.

The main difficulty was that there was only a small power supply to the interior of the mausoleum, and it needed lights to enable us to film it. The solution was to wait until the afternoon when the sun was low enough to shine directly through the pierced marble screens that served as windows. That evening, we got permission to film from one of the minarets, which are normally out-of-bounds and kept locked after several people threw themselves from them. The other members of the crew had already climbed to the top with the aid of a torch, but I had been liaising with the foreman and got there a little later. I was thus forced to climb the stairs in pitch darkness when I noticed a chink of light coming through some wooden shutters at the second level.

Curious and wanting a breather, I opened the shutters to be greeted with the most wonderful sight. The minaret we had chosen to film from was on the west side of the monument, and, in the setting sun, the mausoleum was bathed in a beautiful warm yellow light with pink overtones. I rushed excitedly up the remainder of the steps to the top viewing platform to fetch the Indian photographer who was accompanying us and brought him back down to the window. He was completely overwhelmed and, in his excitement, wanted to get a closer shot, so I had to grab his belt to keep him from falling out over the small balcony.

Afterwards, he told me with tears of emotion in his eyes that he had taken over 12,000 pictures of the Taj Mahal – but this was the best. We did get some amazing and unique panoramic footage from the crypt, the roof and elsewhere that we put on our website, www.taj-mahal.net, together with a score of vignettes telling the story of the monument, and in time the website received millions of visitors. Given the hassle that we had gone through, I doubt, with the enhanced security now in place, that anyone will get a similar chance to film there in future.

My main regret was that as we left on the evening of the final day's filming, the lights were still on inside the monument, and the dome appeared luminescent in the gathering gloom outside; what a picture that would have been, but all our cameras were packed away, and we had to leave urgently in order to catch our flight. In fact, I told our giant Sikh driver that we were in a hurry, and he drove like a madman – several times on the wrong side of the dual carriageway to avoid obstructions such as bullock carts and camels. I discovered that it is a big mistake to ask a Sikh driver to be quick; they do not need any encouragement.

An interesting sidelight on the web, and the prominence of your website in the Google listings, is that when our Taj Mahal website was first put up, it was immediately placed at the top of the listing when you typed in "Taj Mahal". However, in recent years, that position has been usurped by the Wikipedia entry, which has about one-tenth the information that our website has, with some of it wrong, followed by the Trump Taj Mahal hotel in Atlantic City and a blues singer called Taj Mahal (why?), both of which have giveaways in their URLs.

There is also a trivial Taj Mahal news site. Given that most people automatically click on the top one or two entries when surfing the net and don't bother to look further, it is strange that Google, with all their much-vaunted technology and research, have yet to come up with an algorithm that places a website more prominently if it actually deals with the subject requested, rather than obvious commercial spin-offs/rip-offs of the name.

Even Yahoo, MSN and Bing do better than this, so it can't be impossible. Heaven forbid that Google search outcomes should be influenced by commercial considerations, which surely can't be, aren't their profits large enough already, and doesn't their corporate philosophy adjure them not to do evil and injure people? But it was always thus – when you get to be a virtual monopoly, you don't give a shit, or put more politely – Power corrupts. Absolute power corrupts absolutely.

One thing is for certain; just as with Microsoft, its operating system and browser, which was allowed by the US government to plough all competition such as Netscape into the ground, on the basis that they may have been a monopoly, but they were our monopoly, nothing will be done about it in the good old USA.

In fact, it took the European Commission to actually face up to Microsoft, levy hundreds of millions of euros in fines for their anti-competitive practices, and finally force Microsoft to unbundle their browser from their operating system. The reality is that big money fixes the outcomes of commercial conflicts in the US courts, and no one, and nothing but a government organisation, can take on a big monopoly like Microsoft or Google – and even then, when several US judges ruled against Microsoft, their findings were overturned in "higher" courts.

Google is potentially a really dangerous Big Brother-type organisation as it keeps records of all searches using Google for months, if not years – so never use Google to ask for sensitive information, get the actual website names you need by another route – you have been warned.

My own experience of the US legal system was limited to a spat with our American distributor for Foul Play, Educorp, who tried to renege on a contract to take thousands of copies of the product for the US market. Fortunately we had passed the proposed contract through one of the top US law firms, Baker Donelson, which had been founded by my business partner's uncle in conjunction with the statesman and politician James Baker.

Their people had recommended several changes to the "standard" Educorp contract, which in the event prevented Educorp from later walking away from the deal and made it prohibitively expensive for them to go to court as it was to be adjudicated under the laws of Delaware, thousands of miles from the Educorp HQ in California.

Thanks to my partner, we also bested the Hearst Corporation, doyen of US newspaper publishing, who had objected to our filing for a trade mark for "Virtual Travel" in the US when we had already secured it in the UK. They had a travel website they wanted to use it for, but William D. brilliantly suggested that if they objected to our filing – for the purposes we had in mind, i.e. our technology, it would leave the name open for anyone to use, which would be against Hearst's interests. They saw the logic in this and agreed to our trademark if they could also use it for their purposes too. Game over.

Oman – The Last Crusade?

I and my wife had been asked in 2000 to stay in Oman by an old friend, Major-General Robin Searby, who at the time was the senior British liaison officer to the Sultan and had been in my regiment. He subsequently left the Army and worked in a private capacity for one of the major trading companies in Oman, and I suggested to him that it might be worth investigating whether the Ministry of Information – later Tourism – would be interested in funding a virtual tour of Oman for their website to replace the rather poor images and web presentation describing the main tourist locations in Oman.

The idea was that the company, Bahwan, would contract with the Ministry for the work and pass the project on to us. I went out to Muscat in 2004 to do a presentation to the Ministry in the company of three senior people from Bahwan, including Hind, the beautiful daughter of old Suhail Bahwan. She was the chief executive officer of the company and a friend of the lady Minister of Tourism, who chaired the meeting.

With the benefit of hindsight (no relation), the seeds of our future problems were sown the moment I tried to connect to the Ministry's Internet connection to download panoramas from our Taj Mahal website because it was so slow that I had to revert to an offline copy of the site on a disc I had brought with me. Naturally, I explained what had happened and why we were offline, not realising that I had unwittingly caused the consultant, an Egyptian called

Tariq, who had installed it, to lose a serious amount of face in front of his clients, the Ministry.

Perhaps not surprisingly, he weighed in and asked lots of, mostly stupid, questions, which I answered happily, with him getting noticeably more het-up. Meanwhile, another member of the Ministry, a lady called Abeer, asked some relevant and sensible questions, which showed that, unlike Tariq, she had a good grasp of the technology, much experience in tourism and a serious interest in the project. The Minister let all this pass without comment and engaged in some banter with Hind, who showed her an amusing cartoon strip that I had on my mobile.

The meeting ended with apparent satisfaction on the part of the Bahwan contingent, and I was asked to quote a price for the project. Some weeks later, I heard that our quotation had been accepted but that they were not ready to sign a contract. With Bahwan's encouragement I flew out to Muscat shortly before Christmas 2004 and arranged to spend several days there filming in order to get the project underway, as well as meeting the Deputy Minister.

I had asked them for a list of sites to film, even suggesting some that I knew were interesting and photogenic, and though a list was eventually sent to me, it clearly did not represent the best tourism or most attractive sites to take images, though some obvious locations that I had suggested were included.

On arrival in Oman, Bahwan provided me with a small 4WD vehicle and a charming Omani driver, and we raced around the countryside within a day's drive of Muscat, taking panoramic images in a dozen or so places. Two days later, back in Muscat, I met with the deputy Minister and Tariq and showed them some digital images of the places we had been to and emphasised that we were serious about the project and wished to get it underway as soon as possible. Tariq was extremely rude to me in front of the Minister, hoping, I suspect, that I would be so offended that I would back off the project.

The Minister smoothed it over but it was obvious that Tariq was trying to sabotage the project and had taken violent objection to me. I left Oman the next day with nothing further resolved, but before I left, Robin Searby, who had kindly had me stay in his lovely house on the outskirts of Muscat, warned me that the Omani hierarchy depended on outside workers like Tariq, the Egyptian, and the Indians at Bahwan, who actually did all the work, but were looked down on and given no real responsibility by the Omanis.

Worse still, all real power still resided in the hands of the Sultan, who was regarded as a demi-god and who nobody dared to gainsay – except Searby when he was still in the Army there. Like most consultants, Tariq did not actually do any real work either, or judging by the Internet connection fiasco, none that was effective, and was really only interested in protecting his position.

Anyway, we, or at any rate Bahwan, did manage to get the contract signed a few months later with an initial down payment, and I went out there again to take more photographs, some on their list, some suggested by me, based on what I had noted on my earlier visits.

After much badgering, I got permission to film in the enormous Grand Mosque in Muscat and took a tripod that was extendable up to 25 feet so that I could include in the panoramas a view of the beautiful and amazing Persian carpet 70 metres square, containing 1.7 billion stitches. This was a precarious and chancy operation in the extreme because I was not allowed to take a ladder into the Mosque, and the camera had to be level so that the ends of the panoramic image matched up. Anyway I levelled the camera on its adjustable head, extended all the legs to their maximum and prayed for the best as I used the remote control to take the shot.

I also got permission to take a picture from the top of the Mirani fort overlooking the Sultan's palace and harbour in Muscat. This picture needed much work in Photoshop as the back of the roof contained a huge satellite dish with my accompanying guard crouched behind it, though very much visible. The next day, I flew down to Salalah in the south of the country to film the frankincense trees and the beaches, and then up to Musandam at the very northern tip of the country to film a fort and the mountains and beaches there.

187

Having done all this, I then had another meeting with the Ministry, showed them some of the images, received more unhelpful comments from Tariq and returned to the UK. William D. then put all the images up on a website for them to see, and a week or so later, I received a letter from the Ministry saying that many, if not most, of the images were unacceptable. I had, in the meantime, sent them the scripts that I had written both for the audio to accompany the panoramas and also to accompany the movies to explain the history and culture of the country.

Sensibly, we decided to 'pretty up' the panoramas in Photoshop and eventually received a grudging admission that many, but not all of them, were OK. For the others, they refused to say why they did not like them or what places we should have shot instead and made no comment at all on the scripts. They then said they wanted to terminate the contract, so I flew out again at 24 hours' notice but missed the meeting because my plane was four hours late.

I tried to get Hind to ask her friend at the Ministry to put Ms Abeer in charge of the project rather than Tariq, but Hind refused to do so. The wrangling went on with Tariq until a conference call was arranged with him, during which he demanded that I come out to Oman for at least six weeks to take more photographs. He obviously knew that I would never accede to that demand without any commitment that he would approve them, and I then discovered, because he mistakenly sent me an e-mail addressed to a photographic studio in Oman, that he had arranged with the latter to have them take photographs instead.

I wrote to the Minister, copying the letter and complaining about his underhand tactics, but the contract was cancelled anyway. Not a happy experience for all concerned, and in the end, the Ministry lost out as they had paid a deposit, got nothing for it, and were unable, as it turned out, to improve their website, which looked awful, if you could get it to load at all. And all because of Tariq – the wrecker – and consultant.

We went confidently into the deal because we had a good friend in Robin at Bahwan, a major trading company there. I got on well with all the people in Bahwan (who were all mad about cricket, like me). We had a great product and an excellent track record making these virtual tours, and clearly, the Omani Ministry of Tourism needed to improve their website or portal. However, these advantages counted as nothing when set against a consultant who was determined to cover up his incompetence and get part of the action for his photographer friends.

The fact that he was supported by the Ministry merely shows how feeble they were – result... everyone lost. Ironically, one of the people from the Ministry – an Omani – did offer to help me, and we took some great photographs (rejected by Tariq, needless to say) when he accompanied me to the mountains. Should I have tried to have Ms. Abeer put in charge of the project at that initial meeting?

Probably, but I did not then realise how malicious Tariq was, and obviously, I did not want to offend people there whom I had never previously met.

In retrospect, it would have saved everyone a lot of time and money if I had simply said to the Minister, "Why is this man in charge of this project? Because he clearly knows nothing of the technology, nor the geography, nor tourism in Oman and so there is no point in my working with him. However, Ms. Abeer appears to have all those qualities." Rude – but right. They would then have either to ditch the project, dump me, or hand over control of it to Ms. Abeer. Any of those outcomes would have been preferable to what actually happened.

The only upside was that I took some wonderful pictures of a beautiful country, which we have been able to use subsequently.

Gardens – Is Everything in them Rosy?

In 1999, suggested by Nicky Gowland, we decided to undertake a project on Kew Gardens and began negotiations with them to enable us to produce a CD-ROM and website. The rationale was that they are probably the world's best-known gardens, there was no virtual tour of them (that we knew of), and we reckoned that the development costs would be relatively low as we could use the code that had been created for us for the Taj Mahal website and because Kew was only 15 minutes drive from the office, so filming would be easy and inexpensive. The marketing of the website and selling of the CD-ROM would be done in conjunction with Kew who would promote it on their own website and sell the product in their shop.

Taking the panoramic pictures at Kew was a continuing joy as we filmed different parts of the 300-acre landscape at different times to bring out their best features or when, for example, the bluebells were out. We were also very lucky in that we received the assistance of Ray Desmond, who had written the definitive history of Kew a few years earlier. He also helped point us in the right direction to get pictures and information from their extensive archives and in writing/editing the script for the vignettes describing the historic buildings, such as the Palm House, and people, like Sir Joseph Banks, who had taken a major role in Kew's development.

We also got much help from the staff there who found us, for example, a plant discovered and described by Charles Darwin in his own hand and held in the records of the Herbarium. Touchingly, Emma, who ran the Palm House, showed us, with tears in her eyes, a little plant with white flowers that was the last surviving member of its species. We were also treated to a tour of the immense compost heap, the largest in Europe, apparently, that helps keep the gardens in their flourishing state.

As usual I got rather carried away and produced more material than was strictly necessary, which caused something of a problem when we were attempting to get the scripts approved by people at Kew. I had been rather critical of the painting of the exterior of Kew Palace by English Heritage, a sort of terracotta red, and apparently, that had not gone down too well. I had a point, as Ray Desmond agreed, in that EH said their reason for doing so was that that had been the original colour. This is disputed by the experts. Anyway, we finally got the script approved and recorded, using the wonderful voice, as always, of Nicolette Mckenzie, whom we had first used on Foul Play.

In due course, the disc went on sale in the shop, and when I met the marketing lady there, called, I believe Alison, she agreed that we could have a banner on the Kew Gardens' homepage and a link to our virtual tour website as we had agreed in the contract. Subsequent to the meeting, I was unable to get hold of her for several weeks, though I had written a nice letter to her summarising the agreements in the meeting and thanking her for her help.

Eventually, I heard from another source that someone connected with Kew had done an academic-oriented virtual tour of the gardens some years before using very poor technology and at nothing like the width or depth that we had achieved. I heard that, apparently, she felt that that absolved her and Kew from any responsibility to carry out their side of the bargain as agreed in the contract, presumably because she did not want to tread on their peoples' toes.

I complained to all and sundry, but it was clear that we were not going to get anywhere, and so we were forced to put up with nothing but a few words on the Kew website for a few weeks, mentioning our virtual tour. Very disappointing, but I did get several orders for reasonable numbers of the CD-ROM disc – which had been well reviewed in the Gardening Press – after I installed a kiosk system outside their shop to demonstrate the programme and allow members of the public to try the virtual tour.

This led us on to the idea of producing a Gardens Directory of the best gardens in the UK, and I put the idea to Jeremy Westwood, an old friend whom I had met at Bartholomew in Edinburgh when we were discussing the Virgin World Digital Mapping project in the early 1990s. He was now running Insight Guides, which produced illustrated travel guides for hundreds of cities and countries worldwide. He was keen on the idea and put up some funding so that we could produce a website and printed illustrated guide to the best three or four hundred gardens in the UK and Ireland.

I had previously gone to Bloomsbury who, at that time, published the Good Gardens Guide, the leading printed UK garden directory, and although I got good support from a very nice guy there called Bill Swainson, unfortunately, the editor and owner of the material called Peter Lloyd, was not so helpful and effectively cancelled the contract that we had laboriously negotiated, even though it had already been signed by Bloomsbury. I got a letter of apology from the managing director of Bloomsbury; not that that helped much.

Anyway, we managed, with some difficulty, to get images from all of the gardens that we wanted to include, wrote up the descriptions from a variety of sources, included much additional material, such as nearby hostelries and attractions, and sent it off to Insight Guides, who scanned the images in Singapore and returned us digital copies.

Inevitably, some images got lost in the process, which led to a bit of friction with one or two of the gardens, and I found myself disputing the matter with a particular garden in the court at Norwich. Fortunately, the judge saw my point, which was that the valuation of over £3,000 for two images was absurd since the garden claimed to have a library of many thousands of images but only received income of a few pounds per image. I agreed to pay them £50, which, if anything, was on the generous side.

William Donelson, as usual, did an excellent job completing the website and laying out all the data in a simple but easy-to-follow manner, with various ways of searching for the garden you want, and we get a thousand plus visitors a day to www.gardens-guide.com.

However, it took much longer for Insight Guides to produce the book, and unfortunately, they missed the boat that year because most garden guides come out in January or thereabouts, and theirs arrived just in time for the Chelsea Flower Show in May. Compared with its competitors, it contained far more pictures – all of high quality – and much better maps and additional information. Undoubtedly, the writing was not as finely crafted as The Good Gardens Guide, but there was obviously not time for us to visit all 400+ gardens and write them up, though I did edit out the more commercial statements that some of them sent us in their descriptions of their gardens.

We did do a regular annual update, which was, I believe, more frequent than most, if not all, of the competing directories. One of the joys of producing the directory was the glorious uncertainty of the response that you sometimes got when you rang to chase up the garden owner, many of whom were pretty eccentric, to say the least.

One lady in the Borders answered my query for a picture of her beautiful garden by telling me that she had unfortunately broken her leg falling down the stairs, was laid up in bed on the ground floor and so could not dig out any photographs until it got better and she could rummage about upstairs. She then treated me to a long dissertation on the horrors of farming in the Borders, what with the bad weather they had been getting that year. If you live in the Borders, can you expect any other kind of weather?

We also arranged with a number of gardens to take panoramic images to put on the website, with Helmingham Hall and the rhododendron gardens at Bowood standing out as being particularly stunning. I was asked to take panoramas at Powerscourt and Annesley Gardens in Ireland and managed to make a small profit on the deal by flying over and filming both of them on the same day – unfortunately, a rainy one, but what do you expect in Ireland? That meant that I had to race down to Wicklow and then back up to Castlewellan in County Down before getting back to the airport.

The rainy weather did mean that I had both gardens pretty much to myself which made taking the photographs easier and quicker. I also had an alarming trip to the Castle of Mey, the late Queen Mother's castle, which is on the northern tip of Scotland. Fortunately, it was a nice sunny day but very windy, which is typical of that part of the world, and I had to film with the tripod extended to its maximum. This was because the garden has many tall internal hedges, as well as a high garden wall, to protect the plants from the salt-laden sea breezes. Twenty-five feet up a rickety ladder, I was not so well protected and several times almost took a header into the rose bushes when buffeted by a strong gust.

To cap it all, I was told that I could get up on top of the potting shed through a skylight, but as I was balancing on a plastic milk crate with the camera in one hand halfway through the open skylight, the crate shot away from under me, and the heavy skylight lid crashed down on my hand. Obviously, I could not let go of the camera, so I somehow managed to use my head and shoulders to lift the lid sufficiently to release my hand and start over. As might be expected, when I did finally get up on the roof, the view was not really worth it.

The Castle of Mey is an amazing place, and if you are ever in those parts – which is highly unlikely – it is well worth visiting. There is, frankly, nothing else up there, and I could understand the frustration and boredom of a friend who was a courtier and obliged to go there to look after the Queen Mother when she visited it each year. She required all the courtiers to get out of the Castle every afternoon, supposedly for a walk, but I believe he spent the time in the nearest betting shop, as you would.

During our period of garden mania, we got permission from the Royal Horticultural Society to film at the Chelsea Flower Show and Hampton Court Flower Show in 2003. This was quite tricky to do as it involved getting onto the large show stands on the first private view day and taking panoramic images, usually with the public gawping from the viewing end of each stand. The problem with that was that the public were likely to move about and thus produce blurred images.

However, we managed quite successfully and put up the results as part of the www.gardens-guide.com website. The BBC made a big production of the Chelsea show in particular, fronted brilliantly then by Alan Titchmarsh, and I wrote to him after the Chelsea Show pointing out that the BBC's own website showed panoramic images that were clearly much inferior to ours, largely because they used a different technique.

After months of much persuading and back-and-forth, due, I suspect, to some pushing back by their current supplier, I finally got an agreement from them on the Friday before the 2004 Show opened on the following Monday. The problem was that the proprietor of the panoramic technology they were using, called IPIX Corporation, was trying at that time to enforce a US patent that they owned in Europe.

It turned out that they had actually 'borrowed' some of the technology from a German university professor and that, anyway, the patent was not enforceable as it was too all-encompassing and/or there was Prior Art – I possess panoramic images of St. Moritz taken in 1909! In order to get the BBC contract, I was forced to become an ad hoc 'expert' in patent law to counter the ridiculous claims made by the agent for IPIX.

I finally succeeded, but only at the last moment, and then probably only because the other party could not get their act together in time. Amazingly, the BBC lawyers tried to cancel the contract on that Monday, again using the IPIX patent pretext, though I refused to countenance it. Luckily, in-house lawyers are rarely a patch on top lawyers at a large commercial practice. I found that I could usually manage to handle them, even without specific legal help.

In the end, we took the photographs, and they looked a whole lot better than anything done previously with the IPIX system or, indeed, done by the RHS's own people for their website that year. However, because I had been forced to take a hard line with the BBC, they would not use us again, though they did pay their bill. The Chelsea Flower Show element of the BBC's website now has video expositions on each show garden, which is really more up their street and can be used in or derived from their broadcast programmes.

As for IPIX? It went bust in 2006, and most of its assets were purchased by Sony at a knock-down price. IPIX had done an IPO for $347 million but lost it all in the dot.com bust of 2001 and more after that, culminating in an annual loss of $3.8 million in 2006. We used Professor Helmut Dersch's PanoTools technology, PTViewer and Apple's QuickTime VR.

Going to the Movies – Is there a Cure for Cinemania?

In the late 1980s I had been given by my brother-in-law a copy of Halliwell's Film Guide for Christmas and realised that there was an opportunity to create a directory of movies on CD-ROM and add pictures or publicity stills from those movies. I, therefore, contacted Harper Collins, who published Halliwell's in book form every year and met their editor for lunch in a small restaurant off Fulham Palace Road, near Harper Collins' massive headquarters. She was happy for me to purchase the rights for a few thousand pounds, plus royalties, and add images from elsewhere if we could obtain them.

I then approached the British Film Institute (BFI) and a friend who ran a small multimedia company called FitVision. He agreed to find a graphics expert and also follow up on my contact with the BFI, and get as many promotional images from their extensive files as he could manage. We began production on the basis that we would split the profits from the sale of the discs, whose physical production we were funding through a loan from the bank.

FitVision produced quite a clever programme with some interesting and innovative ways to access the film you were looking for if, for example, you only knew the name of the director and/or an actor, or the date of release, etc. Unfortunately, the graphics guy, who was at the Royal College of Art and, I later discovered, on any number of illegal substances, elected to produce an interface with a colour scheme that varied between vomit green and vomit yellow – and then he mysteriously disappeared.

FitVision, who rapidly became known as UnfitVision, largely because of the grossly overweight nature of its proprietor, also decided to produce the programme in Supercard, which was a brilliant idea if you only wanted an Apple Macintosh version but hopeless if you needed a PC version. Sadly we believed the promises that there would be a Supercard PC version, though it never materialised.

We were also somewhat handicapped by the refusal of many of the film distributors or rights owners to allow us to use the images from the BFI. This was completely unexpected as we were, in effect, promoting their films, and I believe they only refused because they did not properly understand what we were doing.

So, in the end, Halliwell's Film Guide on CD-ROM contained details on over ten thousand films with several hundred images and ran on the original classic Apple Mac, as well as on the larger colour version, and we got distribution in the US through Educorp, who specialised in Mac products.

Shortly after this, we heard rumours that Microsoft was about to produce a similar product called Cinemania, which did run on the PC, as you would expect. As you might also expect, its interface was not nearly as good as ours, and the directory on which it was based was a much inferior publication to Halliwell's, but Microsoft promoted it heavily and, not surprisingly, it did sell pretty well.

A year or so later, I found some people in Cambridge who were prepared to produce a PC version, and I approached Harper Collins for permission to extend the licence, which was due to expire in a few months' time. However, their lawyer, who had dealt with the matter previously, was by now due to be replaced by another man who, when I did finally get hold of him, promptly went on three weeks' holiday.

I waited patiently for him to return to his desk, with the licence deadline fast approaching, only to be told that he was re-organising his filing cabinets and could not deal with any other issues for at least a week! By the time he had finished doing this, the licence had expired and Harper Collins refused to renew it, despite my protests. So, we sold off the remaining Mac discs to cover most of our expenses, paying back all but a small part of the original bank loan.

Obviously, this type of product has since been completely supplanted by web-based products, which have the latest releases, as well as details on every film ever made, where they are showing, and all for free. Still, our Halliwell's Guide was one of the first mass-market multimedia products and distinctly better than Cinemania in almost every respect (except the colour scheme!)

I was told that Harper Collins had contracted with a consultant to set up a multimedia publishing operation based on HC properties.

Apparently, they spent some £4.5m on the scheme without producing a single product.

At about that time Microsoft released Encarta, a CD-ROM encyclopaedia based on a very inferior printed work that was very US-oriented. It included a great many maps and pictures, and the friend, John Snyder, who had suggested that his company produce the PC-version of Halliwell's, was also involved with an image database system designed in Cambridge to manage the huge set of images in the Pitt-Rivers Collection. John was invited out to Redmond, Washington, by Microsoft and took his software system on disc with him.

I warned him to be very careful in his dealings with them, but he nevertheless gave the engineers there a copy for evaluation and returned to the UK. He heard subsequently from Microsoft that they did not wish to use his system, though he told me ruefully that something that looked very similar turned up in the next release of Encarta. I heard a year or two later that Encarta, like Cinemania, was discontinued by Microsoft.

In fact, I had approached Encyclopaedia Britannica two years earlier and tried to persuade them to allow me to produce a CD-ROM version, but without success. Spurred on by Encarta, they duly did produce a CD-ROM version in 1994, which sank the company two years later as they had discontinued the 30-odd volume printed version, from which most of their profits came. It turned out that people liked to display their set of the Encyclopaedia in all its beautifully bound glory of multiple volumes in a bookcase – not a visual effect you get with a CD-ROM…

The company was bought out and then split into two in 2001, with one half producing the print version – to proudly display on your shelves (£945) – and the other the DVD-ROM version (£40 p.a). Charles Babbage, the computing pioneer and inventor, was an early fan of Britannica, reading and learning the entire 20-volume set as a child in the early nineteenth century.

John Snyder was a remarkable photographer who had travelled out overland to Timbuktu to photograph the Tuareg tribespeople and, while up-country, had been bitten by a dog that people thought was rabid. He was rushed 400 miles in a Land Rover to Timbuktu to have injections in his stomach and later returned up-country to be told that all he had had to have done was to suck on a date stone that had been in the mouth of a member of a certain local tribe, which apparently conferred immunity. Would you have taken the risk, though?

Travel Guides – Virtually There?

In early 2004, I had an idea that printed travel guides would soon be transposed onto mobile telephones and immediately went out and purchased a Motorola A920 half brick-like phone which had a touch screen, GPS receiver, 320x240 colour screen, hand-writing and speech recognition, a camera, diary, calculator etc. 3-G connection, and a rudimentary on-line guide to restaurants and shops, etc. Sounds familiar?

At that time, the A920 was by far the most advanced phone available and pointed the way to the future, though it has to be said that its features were somewhat difficult to use. I took it along to a meeting I had set up with a well-known travel books publisher, which was run by an old friend of mine – Jeremy Westwood. He was very enthusiastic about the idea, and we agreed to pursue it in whatever way seemed appropriate.

A few weeks later, I attended, as a guest, a meeting organised by and for MiT alumni, of which my business partner William Donelson was one. There, we met someone from Orange, the network operator, who suggested we contact a small German SatNav software company called *gate 5*. They were looking for partners who could provide content as they were in the process of developing a 'plug-in' concept to enable travel guides, amongst other programmes, to knit into their mapping software by using standard interface formats.

In the Spring of 2004, we all met up in the travel guides publisher's offices and agreed to go ahead and put a couple of their guides onto the gate 5 system. Contracts were signed with both the publisher and gate 5 and in due course, we succeeded in getting guides to London and Paris onto the card that by then could be inserted into most of the small number of available smartphones (principally Symbian and Windows products, though not the A920).

Gate 5 was attempting to sell some of the airlines on the idea that you could purchase a smart card in-flight with a guide to your destination city, but it was too early in the product cycle as not nearly enough phones of the right type were available. Nevertheless, gate 5 were doing a good job and seemed to have the technology licked. They did succeed in selling their SatNav product, smart2go, to one or two German motor manufacturers for in-car navigation, which kept the company alive.

They asked us to produce another half-dozen city guides, including one to Barcelona, where the upcoming annual GSM mobile phonefest was due to happen in January 2006. Gate 5 produced a smart card with the City Guide to Barcelona on it and distributed it to all and sundry, which may have had a good effect because later in the autumn of 2006, they announced that Nokia was taking them over for a sum believed to be in the region of €150 million.

However, by this time, the travel guide publisher was becoming lukewarm about the concept and had given up sending us digital versions of their products, which they had done initially under the terms of our contract, as they said it was too difficult. We decided, therefore, that if we were to remain in the Nokia catalogue, we were obliged to scan and digitise the guides ourselves from the books. This involved an awful lot of extra work as we determined to identify and locate every place mentioned in the books, not just those major sights shown on the in-book maps.

This is easy in the developed and well-mapped world but much less so in China and India, for which Nokia were very interested in having products since those countries were a rapidly expanding part of their market. It came down to using Google Earth to physically identify the locations from GE's aerial photography and satellite images, so I can imagine how it must have felt for the analysts trying to identify enemy installations from aerial photographs during WWII.

Occasionally, Wikimapia would provide a clue, but it featured so many locations that were of a personal nature, such as "Anil's girlfriend's house", that the time spent on it was usually wasted. It is interesting that the owners of Wikipedia are at last taking steps to prevent correct content on living or reasonably contemporary people being altered for malicious or facetious reasons, but my experience is that if you do happen to find content that you know for certain is wrong, it is nearly impossible to correct it and ensure that your corrections stick.

This makes Wikipedia a very unreliable source and it is therefore infuriating that the Wikipedia item for any given subject nearly always features near the top of the relevant Google listing. Lazy journalists frequently use Wikipedia, and information is therefore widely propagated that is completely wrong but nevertheless gaining extra credence from being quoted afresh and thus becoming, in many people's eyes, a fact. As usual, we are heading rapidly for Lowest Common Denominator information rather than Highest Common Factor, though I am pretty sure neither of those concepts is taught in Maths in schools nowadays.

Google Maps is fine for identifying locations and giving the Longitude and Latitude in the Western World, though Multimap used to be very helpful until the company was taken over by Microsoft and the interface 'modernised', thereby eliminating some of its most useful features, but now including much irritating advertising. The country maps in the travel guide books were often at too large a scale to be of much use in identifying a hotel in a small town, for example, and I found quite a few errors in the city maps.

A reference to Google Maps also showed that if the place was a restaurant, for instance, it was still open and gave its correct telephone number, which was frequently wrong in the book. Using all these tools, we rapidly compiled a catalogue of all the major cities that were tourist/business destinations and began producing a number of country-wide guides where there were too many cities – for example, England – to be worth selling as individual products. For Malaysia or India, the tourist locations were widely dispersed around the country, so city guides were not of much interest.

Nokia gate 5 launched the N95 mobile with Nokia Maps in mid-2007, but unfortunately for us, they had been concentrating, not surprisingly, on the usability of the Maps element of the software rather than the accessibility of the catalogue of travel guides, with the outcome that nobody but a real mobile nerd would have been prepared to spend the time finding and purchasing the travel guides.

The net result was, therefore, that sales were perhaps a tenth of what we had been expecting, and so we complained bitterly to Nokia that it was not reasonable to expect users to go through endless menus to find a travel guide and that when they did so, there was no way of discovering what content a specific guide included. For example, one well-known brand of travel guides in the Nokia catalogue featured 100 or fewer points of interest (POIs) of all types, e.g. 20 sights, 20 hotels, 20 restaurants, etc. which is clearly insufficient for Paris, for example; whereas others (including ours) featured a thousand or more POIs for the same destination.

Nokia took almost a year to fix this with a newer version of Maps, but competition, such as Google Maps on mobiles, had appeared like dragons' teeth in the meantime, and much of the early momentum had been lost as SatNav became a relatively common feature on smart mobiles.

It is also true that, for the most part (pre-Waze), people did not use a SatNav system very frequently, i.e. less than once a month, unless they were taxis, delivery drivers or travelling salesmen, in which case they usually had a dedicated in-car system. They were, therefore, unlikely to be bothered to invest much time and effort in getting used to a SatNav system on their mobile unless it was going to pay dividends on holiday or on a business trip, and if they didn't use the SatNav, they would not get to, nor need, the travel guide, especially if they had to pay an extra £6 or so for it, on top of the navigation licence cost.

In fact, there have really only been a couple of occasions when I really needed the SatNav system on my N95 mobile; once, my wife needed to find a friend's house in deepest Northumberland and the other in Ireland for a wedding. On the latter occasion, SatNav was absolutely vital as we went from church to reception and then to the house we were staying in near Limerick, mostly in darkness and without any road signs, which the Irish obviously think are an unnecessary distraction!

On arriving back at the house where we were staying ("You have now reached your destination!"), it was 3 am, pitch dark and the front door was locked, so I used the lit-up element of my mobile's screen to find my way through the garden to the back door. As I had previously used the N95's camera to capture images and video of the happy couple, as well as making several phone calls and getting e-mails via a website, I had, on that one trip, used most of my mobile's multimedia features – at last!

The point is that that weekend was really an exception, which I guess applied for most people, most of the time. However, it did mean that I did not need to carry a camera in my morning coat, hire an unfamiliar SatNav system with the car, trip over the rockery in the darkness, borrow my host's computer (if he had had one), or use his 'phone. Not bad value, really for a device costing £30 a month – with all calls for free.

So the conclusion is that, for most people, the SatNav system and City/Country guides on a mobile are really only useful when you are doing something out of the norm, i.e. on a holiday or business trip. This means that people will be unwilling to pay for these extra facilities, which in turn means that the costs of providing them can only be recouped through advertising.

Obviously, Nokia and Apple and co. are unwilling to be the salesman/agent for advertisers, so their strategy must be to provide app stores where people can find and download – usually for free – the content, such as travel guides, that they want. This is indeed happening, and it is now a common occurrence to download the maps, guides, weather, traffic, etc., for the area that you are travelling to or have just flown in to.

The travel guide includes panoramic images that are much larger than the mobile display but which scroll left/right and up/down and describe in audio the sight(s) that you are seeing. You can also click on hotspots in the picture to get more (audio) information about specific landmarks that you can see. The panoramic image is linked to travel guide information such as the telephone number (for automatic dialling), address, dates and times of opening, cost and detailed text description.

However, to return to the situation with Nokia and our publisher, in early 2008 I persuaded the travel guides people to ante up some cash in order to include pictures from their archive and to allow us to update the guides. It turned out that they did not have digital copies or digital versions of many of the cities that we needed and, so we had to have the transparencies scanned – somewhat inadequately – and it proved a nightmare to identify many of the POIs that had been photographed, even when they had been done with a digital camera fairly recently.

In fact, the whole thing was a mess, and it took us ages to get the images from the publisher, identify them, process them and include them in the Nokia catalogue, and even then, we only got images for about 50% of the Cities/Countries that we wanted. Annoyingly, on examining the recently commissioned digital images, we would find that there were about 50 for a particular bar and it was obvious that the photographer had ensconced himself there for the evening and probably taken advantage of the situation to get himself free drinks!

In fact, almost the only city where that had not happened was Taipei, where the photographer seemed to be a bit more honest and did actually get out and photograph all the sights without resorting to fancy/fashionable/bizarre angles, which we found were a real problem to make look right on the small mobile screen.

We encountered a further problem in the lead-up to the Beijing Olympics because we were the only provider of a travel guide to Beijing in the Nokia catalogue and were confidently looking forward to some decent sales as a result. However, a month before the Olympics, we were suddenly informed by Nokia that all the GPS locations we had laboriously identified for Beijing and its environs were wrong.

We investigated why they claimed this was so and discovered that the Chinese authorities had unilaterally decided to use a slightly different mapping system called DITU, which put our GPS locations an average of about 1.5 kilometres out. However, we could not simply apply an offset to correct them as the error varied for each location. I, therefore, had to check and correct every single *Place of Interest*, aided by some clever software that William Donelson produced to speed up the process.

I also had to go through the same process for the Shanghai and Hong Kong products to which the same problem applied. By dint of working all hours we managed to get the three cities corrected and returned to Nokia in less than ten days. However, they were somewhat reluctant to incorporate them in their catalogue as they did not believe that we could have done it so quickly. Eventually, they did agree a few days before the opening of the Olympics and put the products back online.

A couple of days later, a Chinese publisher objected that we had the wrong locations for a couple of hotels in Beijing, and our product was again withdrawn from the Nokia catalogue. I checked the data and discovered that one hotel they had complained about was actually correctly positioned, and the other was only about 200 metres out, though as it was 300 feet high, it would have been clearly visible from about a kilometre away.

I also discovered that the publisher who had complained had had their own product incorporated in the Nokia catalogue not long before! I got right back to Nokia with the corrected data and a complaint that we had been unfairly treated. Nokia reacted reasonably quickly and put our product back in the catalogue, but by then, the Olympics were almost over. The Chinese publisher's product was later withdrawn completely, soon after the Olympics were finished. Nevertheless, they had stuffed us.

The travel guides situation became increasingly fraught in the summer of 2008, and I realised that we were in danger of not making the cut and remaining in the catalogue when Nokia moved on to the next version of their Maps software. I, therefore, wrote to the publisher asking for a meeting and pointing out that they were in breach of our contract by not providing digital content.

That led, in due course, to a rather tricky meeting with their new managing director, who had replaced my friend Jeremy as he had recently retired, who wanted to review the situation and perhaps terminate the contract. I persuaded them to wait until the next set of royalty figures came from Nokia, which would be the first following the release of Maps 2.0, which had turned out to be a distinct improvement on the Maps 1.0 version.

Insight Guides then admitted that they had no means of providing us with digital material as all of their books were published without any database system being involved. I offered to provide one but they said that was impossible, even though we had, in effect, already created one. They then wrote to me asking me to provide a digital copy of all the material we had created, with the obvious objective of stealing it.

During this period there was also a difficult situation developing with both the publisher and Nokia because the publisher had refused to sign a new contract reflecting the changed situation after the take-over of gate 5 by Nokia. I suggested that Armchair Travel sign a contract with Nokia instead, as we already had a contract with the travel guide publisher, but the publisher was unhappy with that, so I then suggested a contract with their international publisher owners.

That proved impossible, so Nokia and ourselves went ahead and eventually agreed and signed a contract at the end of 2008. This contract was approved by the main Nokia board, despite the strictures of the Sarbanes-Oxley Act in the USA, which has the effect of forbidding major corporations from contracting with very small outfits, such as ourselves, for large-scale contracts, all of which shows the importance that Nokia attached to the deal with us. Bear in mind that at that time, Nokia had 40% of the mobile phone market.

In the New Year of 2009, the publisher demanded a meeting, at which, in spite of a 60% increase in our sales figures and thus contrary to their earlier promise, they stated that they were terminating our contract. I was furious about this and demanded to know why, only to be told that the content we had created was, as far as they were concerned, completely out of date, even for books that had been published just a month or two ago. I pointed out that that was nonsense because we had checked and updated all the material in recent months and sent it to Nokia. They refused to relent, and I told them that we would sue them.

This rapidly became a very messy situation because our contract with Nokia could not be fulfilled if the publisher did not provide us with the content, and to make matters worse, the publisher's managing director had not bothered to read her e-mails, nor the contract, so tried to terminate it immediately. I was forced to point out that that would be yet another breach of contract and that it could not be terminated until the end of 2009.

I offered to settle the matter amicably with no costs payable on either side and with us providing them with a small royalty to be able to continue using the digitised content, only to receive a rude telephone call from the publisher's managing director suggesting that we were doing this because we had "run out of money". I pointed out that we had made a profit in our latest published accounts while refraining to mention that they had made a loss of about £100,000 in theirs.

This telephone call, together with the other errors and stupid mistakes that the publisher had made, indicated to me that their M.D. had lost the plot and so I decided that we would initiate a legal action against them. Fortunately, I was able to call on the services of a splendid lawyer from Herbert Smith, who definitely did not lose the plot and indeed produced the most devastating letter that I had ever seen – truly an Exocet of a missive.

This was followed by another even more impressive response to the publisher's rather feeble reply, which had contained numerous errors of fact and misunderstandings, deliberate or otherwise, including the inability to multiply a figure by two. A feature of our lawyer's letters was his characterising of our opponent's arguments as "hopeless", which made his missives very enjoyable to read.

A further exchange of letters took place during which the publisher effectively admitted their breach of contract and offered to settle, although for far too small a sum to compensate us adequately for our efforts. Our lawyer countered with an offer to settle for a figure that would recognise the years of effort we had put into the project.

The publisher then clearly took advice from a junior barrister, who advised them not to respond to our letter unless we were prepared to pay for the time they took to put together a response. We replied with an offer to go to professional legal mediation, only to receive another blocking reply, albeit with a marginally increased offer and a threat that if we wanted a detailed reply, its cost would be deducted from the amount offered.

Our – wonderful lawyer – not two words that you hear coupled together very often, at least from me – was in two minds as to whether we should accept the offer, but I wrote to him saying that up to now, we had been on the same playing field as the publisher, with our lawyer (him) regularly putting the ball past their incompetent goalie of a solicitor.

"I don't think much of their defence"

They had now elected to remove themselves from

the field and were shouting at us from the sidelines. I wanted them back on the field again, so we decided to respond by demanding that they actually answer the points that we had raised, regardless of the threat of paying their costs to do so, in order to draw out their responses, which would have to deal with such questions as misrepresentation of their capabilities when signing the contract, multiple breaches of that and another contract, attempted theft of intellectual property, and in the words of the BBC Radio 4 programme "Just a Minute" – Deviation.

When we eventually received their response it became clear that they had dropped the idea of charging us for answering their letter and, to our surprise, now offered to go to mediation. It was obvious in their reply that they had nothing to offer to counter to our accusations of breach of contract, etc. They also managed to trip themselves up by affirming that they had visited the website we had set up to enable them to check our work and then, a couple of paragraphs later, stating that they had no knowledge of the extent of the work we had done in creating City Guides, which also covered the surrounding countryside a day's trip from the city, something that would have been immediately obvious if they had visited the website, as the website displayed a map of the POIs for each city!

Their next ploy was to delay the mediation for a month by writing to us to the effect that the dates they had originally proposed, and to which we had agreed, were no longer possible as they were suddenly going on holiday (which we subsequently discovered was untrue).

After we agreed the new dates, they sent our lawyers two faxes, one a couple of minutes after the other, with two different offers. Our lawyer's comment was "bizarre". On examining them, it became clear that they were trying to drive a wedge between my company and our lawyer by splitting off the costs in offer one – to be negotiated between our lawyer and theirs – and leaving us with a (totally inadequate) lump sum, whereas the second offer was a larger lump sum that included costs. We rejected these and went to mediation as planned and were offered an experienced mediator who had, many years before, been in the same regiment as me. He was known as a good egg, so we snapped him up.

At the mediation, they turned up with their managing director and marketing/rights director, plus the junior lawyer who had been responsible for much of the correspondence and their senior litigation lawyer. So, an expensive day out for them, which indicated that they were taking it pretty seriously. It was arranged that we should all sit round a table to start with and then, if things got contentious, split off into separate rooms. I opened for our side and pointed out in some detail how extensive the process was if we had to create all the material ourselves without any of the help from them which had been specified in the contract – and for which they were getting very substantial royalties.

There were then questions as to why we had not tried to re-negotiate the contract when they stopped sending us digital data. I replied that I believed it was just a temporary problem that prevented them from sending us digital data and updates, which had been confirmed when they told us in mid-2008 that they could not provide us with updates as their systems were inadequate. Their managing director then piped up to say that, of course, they could have provided us with digital data as it was all on discs.

Our lawyer then pointed out that this was a much more serious breach of contract since they had deliberately withheld the data from us and that we could be expected to win damages of the order of several hundred thousand pounds in court when the case went to litigation. Their lawyer then said his piece in response to mine, in which he reverted to their offer of several months back, to which my lawyer replied that in that case, we would have to go to litigation.

The mediator then suggested that I and my lawyer move to another room and that he would get back to us there. After a while he knocked on our door and told us that it was getting very hot and sweaty in our opponents' room, whereas he found ours nice and cool.

We told him that if they did not improve their offer, we would go to litigation since, with this new information, we were certain to win substantial damages and that if we had been given their discs, we would have quickly compiled a catalogue of 150+ products which would have generated substantial royalties both in the past and for the foreseeable future – as it was doing for the electronic travel guides of our competitors.

The only reason that we were still in the building was that we were pretty certain that they were going to go bust in about six months' time, having heard about the recent closure of their printing plant and of their US distributors. After more toing and froing from the mediator, we eventually came to a compromise at the top end of what they could afford and the bottom end of what we could accept. The stench of sweat when we visited their room to sign the agreed settlement document was palpable.

The publishers could have saved everyone a lot of trouble and themselves over £100,000 in costs if they had responded intelligently to my original offer and either accepted it or just paid us off with £20-30,000. I had warned them ten months before that we would sue – and that we would win as we always had with publishers in the past.

However lawyers – even good commercial lawyers – can sometimes be a real pain, as I found out when negotiating an important contract with Lloyds Bank many years before. I had deliberately set the last meeting of many, at which I was seeking final agreement on all outstanding points, for a Friday mid-afternoon, knowing that the bank's staff liked to leave early, if possible, for the weekend.

The clock hands were creeping round to five o'clock, and all points were being agreed at an increasing pace when suddenly our lawyer opened his mouth to raise a fresh issue. I immediately kicked out under the table, and he shut his mouth with a grimace.

Luckily, I was able to distract the bankers' attention, and we signed the agreement and got up to leave, with the lawyer hobbling a little as we went out. He hissed to me, "You didn't have to kick me quite so hard!" I apologised but refrained from telling him that he was taking the punishment for all the irritation that lawyers had caused me down the years.

It is not surprising that Courtroom dramas are so popular because occasionally, a barrister really excels himself, as in a true story that my lawyer told me while we were waiting for the other side to respond during the Mediation mentioned above. My lawyer had been involved in an important case concerning a large TV broadcaster and one of their set-top box contractors who had failed to perform under the contract agreed between the parties.

The foreman of the contractor's installation team was put on the witness stand, and the issue came down to whether his evidence was reliable and trustworthy or was fake. He was boasted about his qualifications and claimed that he had a degree from a university in the Caribbean, which was notorious for issuing degrees via a website without asking for qualifications of any sort.

The broadcaster's QC asked him a series of questions designed to draw out what qualifications he had for obtaining the degree, such as, "Had the foreman visited the university campus?" "*Yes*", "When?", "*Last year*", "How did you get there?" "*I landed on the island airstrip*", "Which lecturers did you meet?" "*I can't remember what they were called*" "What about your fellow students? How many were there?" "*Quite a few, but I don't remember how many*" "So, you were satisfied that this was a genuine university offering reputable degrees to students who had studied at their facility?" "*Yes*".

The Court then adjourned for the weekend, and the broadcaster's lawyers arranged for one of their people to fly to the Caribbean and try to get to the university, which proved to be impossible as the island it was supposed to be located on was uninhabited and had no airstrip, harbour or even a jetty. He contacted the local authorities, who confirmed that the university only existed as a website and that they had been trying to close it down for some years.

On the Monday, the QC, after some further questions to confirm the foreman's confidence in the validity and appropriateness of his degree, produced an impressive-looking document with lots of scroll-work in different colours on it from his briefcase, which he showed to the contractor's foreman and asked him if he recognised it. The foreman said that he did, and when asked why, said it was similar to the one he had obtained from the "*University*". The QC then read out the name of the recipient of the degree from the document, which was "Lulu Dickinson".

He then informed the Court that Lulu Dickinson was obviously very intelligent but probably not capable of getting a degree, as she was his Schnauzer! Some time later I attended a conference in Victoria Street at which I met a man from Sky to whom I recounted this story. He replied that it was very amusing but that he had been involved in the case and had heard that the foreman's company had taken out a contract on him personally, and so he had had to lie low for a year!

Education – Lessons Learned?

In the late 1990s, we determined to attack the education markets, which seemed ready to take CD-ROM products, supported by a Government-backed scheme to fund the purchase of CD-ROMs for schools. We managed to get an excellent distributor called AVP to carry our products, and they started with the Explore Parliament disc, which we soon augmented with a programme on Citizenship developed by a wonderful teacher and courseware developer in Oldham called Cath Wallace.

This was based on the National Curriculum requirements and used elements from the Parliament disc together with new audio, a historical timeline, lesson plans and much else. We tested it thoroughly with a class of a Faith School in Oldham, and amended it where necessary. The class teacher was a superb and inspirational teacher and responded extraordinarily well to the situation. She even arranged a visit for the children to Parliament in London, where their knowledge of the history and contents of the Palace astounded and embarrassed the guide assigned to them when he found himself corrected by 11-year-olds!

I was horrified when introduced to the class to find that there was one extremely bright boy and an equally bright girl in the same class as several very much duller pupils who struggled to grasp even the simplest concepts, with the majority at mid-level. Clearly, this was unfair on all of them – and especially the teacher. But obviously, it would be Politically Incorrect to assign the pupils to different streams, regardless of the fact that they would all benefit.

Our Citizenship programme was the first such course on the market, and we had high hopes for it. Unfortunately, there was both resistance from schools to the implementation of Citizenship as a new element to be shoehorned into the Curriculum, and given that History was being continually downgraded in importance, it clearly went against the grain to use a new history-based product in schools. Nevertheless, we persevered and, in the end, sold quite a few copies of the product.

In the early 2000s, I got into contact with a professor at the University of Florida, called Martin Foys, who had developed a website with the entire Bayeux Tapestry on it using a sideways scrolling mechanism to display all 230 feet of it on-screen, with annotations in English and Latin. He was worried that he would have to pay the French at the Museum in Caen, where the Tapestry was displayed, a fee for the use of the pictures, which he had obtained from a third party.

Fortunately, I heard from a great friend of mine, William Shepherd, an experienced publisher, that there had been a court case in New York where the plea from a British publisher (Bridgeman Art) to claim royalties on images taken of Old Master paintings was thrown out. This breakthrough enabled Martin to create a CD-ROM for sale – as opposed to the free website – and we added some panoramic images to the disc that we took at Senlac Hill, Battle, the site of the Battle of Hastings. The disc was really excellent and an incredible tool for researchers, teachers and students interested in probably the most significant battle (until the Battle of Britain) that has ever taken place in Britain. After all, 1066 is the only historic date that almost everyone in Britain can remember.

We later used the same legal ruling to fight off a claim from a French publisher for royalties on a couple of images – Sher Jahan and Mumtaz Mahal – that we had used in the Taj Mahal project and which had been provided by them, though obviously, we paid their reproduction and transmission costs.

In 2002, I was approached out of the blue by a guy called Edmond Lee, who worked for Gallimard Bayard in Paris to be the distributor of a series of discs called the "First Discovery of Science", which was designed for Primary School children and included wonderful programmes on The Bird, The Frog, The Ladybird and The Tree. The original book versions, beautifully drawn and executed, were translated into 25 languages and sold 40 million copies worldwide.

The CD-ROM versions maintained the same high standards and included excellent animations and very neat games and puzzles to test the user's knowledge. They compared very favourably in content, learning style and attractiveness with offerings from the BBC and other UK publishers aimed at the British market, which were mostly very poor quality drawn cartoons, stepping laboriously through the subject in the dullest way possible, with no sound and almost no animation worth looking at.

After much effort, we finally managed to get them reviewed by the Times Educational Supplement, only to find that the reviewer (a teacher) totally ignored most of their best features and stated that "the language was certainly not appropriate for 4-6 year-olds" and that "a teacher would need to guide the children through this software's navigation rather than simply let them explore".

In the first instance, it is hardly likely that the publishers would have sold millions of the book versions in countless languages if the language was not appropriate for the relevant age group, and in the second instance, we had tested the product thoroughly in a number of schools with the said age group and different teachers and received rave reviews. Isn't it a basic requirement of a good teacher that they guide their children rather than let them just mess about?

He also commented that our company was "an unlikely candidate for publishing education software sources" as if that was at all relevant, and a comment which totally ignored the fact that we had been publishing software for schools for many years. Prejudice seems to be an abiding failing of the teaching profession.

We did, however, get an excellent review of the Bayeux Tapestry disc from a librarian's magazine and soldiered on with all these educational products, selling them quite happily to schools through AVP and getting no negative feedback at all. To complement the Bayeux Tapestry disc, we produced a website for Osprey Publishing for the 1,000th-year anniversary of the Battle of Hastings, which included the panoramas and images of soldiers dressed as they would have been on the day, but most importantly, a time/distance animation showing Harold's astonishing march up to York to fight off the Vikings at Stamford Bridge, before returning south again to counter William the Bastard. Roughly 400 miles, with an army, in 40 days.

I had not realised until I did the research just what a near-run thing the Battle of Hastings was. If the English had held out for just another half-hour, having defended doggedly all day, darkness would have fallen, and William would have been forced to withdraw with all his troops; he would have lost the battle, and the whole early history of England would have been completely different, and arguably better, as the feudal system the Normans imported was a severely retrograde step and much less democratic than the Anglo-Saxon regime. Looks like not much has changed over the Channel.

The fortunes vested on the Norman invaders by William are still a real factor in the land ownership of England today, with some 30% of the total land area still owned by descendants of the Normans. Of course, if you are granted thousands of acres, which you don't have to pay for and don't pay taxes on for hundreds of years, it does make it easier to hang on to.

In due course, the Government's CD-ROM in Schools scheme, like all good things, came to an end, AVP went bust, and we stopped selling any more discs to education. Was it all worthwhile? I suppose the answer must be yes, given that we had at least shown what good educational programmes can do and maybe educated thousands of children who, as a result, will hopefully know more about history, democracy and science than they would have done if we had not made the effort. At least we could be proud of the quality of the programmes, which were considerably better than the norm, e.g. those from the BBC, and maybe raised a few sights for a few people.

Confucius put it something like this: "If you shoot for the stars and hit the moon, it's OK. But you've got to shoot for something. A lot of people don't even shoot."

National Trust – me I'm a decent sort of guy...

Why is it such a pain dealing with organisations that do not have, as their main focus, a profit motive? You would have thought, after all the trouble we had had with the Church of England in the guise of St. Paul's and Westminster Abbey, that we would have approached what looked like the gift horse that the National Trust offered us in the guise of an invitation to tender for a series of virtual tours of their houses in mid-2005, with some caution.

But no, innocent lambs to the slaughter as always, we leapt in and quickly discovered just why the NT have such a bad reputation when it comes to business dealings of any kind. I had heard that they were a nightmare to deal with if you were a stately homeowner who had bequeathed your property to them and provided an endowment to support it, but I never realised just how devious they could be.

Anyway, we received this invitation to tender – having for years sent them discs and information about our systems and products (at their request) – which specified all the features that we commonly included in our virtual tours, 360° panoramas, audio, narrated slideshows, video, maps, simple human interface etc. In fact, the lot. They had not asked for any costings, so we answered it in glee and fully expected to be invited to proceed to the next short-list stage.

So it was with dismay that we heard from a Steve Atkinson that "Although your tours are very full of functionality, we do not think they offer the kind of visitor experience or accessibility requirements that we are looking for." Given that our tours were then in daily use by thousands of people on the Internet, at kiosks at a number of high-traffic heritage sites such as Kew Gardens, St. Paul's, the Historic Dockyards, etc. and in daily use in homes and schools, it seemed completely illogical to slate us for lack of accessibility, or a poor user experience, given that anybody can simply walk up to our tours and use them immediately, with no prior knowledge or instruction.

Obviously, he was not looking for very full functionality either, though clearly, if you have the functionality, you can turn parts of it off if desired. If the functionality is not there in the first place, it is usually a problem to include it.

I strongly objected to being sidelined and wrote to a number of people at the NT, one of whom told me that they were particularly keen on a couple of companies that were strong on systems for the disabled. As we had one of the best kiosk systems in the country for the disabled at Chatham, and all our systems were happily used by the disabled, this was obvious nonsense.

Upon questioning Atkinson on the telephone, it became apparent that neither he nor any of his colleagues had actually tried any of our products/systems, so how could they know whether they were good for the disabled, or anyone else for that matter? I cast many aspersions on the ability of Atkinson to evaluate the tenderers as he seemed neither to know nor be interested in what they were planning.

My pressure did eventually have the effect of getting us back onto the list of tenderers for the next round, only to find that we were again eliminated at the next stage. I then got really angry and contacted a friend who had inherited a large estate in Nottinghamshire and was one of the NT Council Members. He promised to look into it but was snowed by the organisation and came back to me with a rather limp reply saying, in effect, that he could do nothing. By chance, I later discovered that one of the National Trust gardens, Nymans, had been beautifully photographed, and the photographs were used in a stunning virtual tour created by an independent photographer.

I called him and discussed his virtual tour, to be told that he had only been contacted by the National Trust **one day** before the tender was due to be returned, which obviously made it impossible for him to submit a reply. I wrote to my contact on the National Trust Council and pointed this out, together with a comment that, in my experience, it looked as if it was an "insider" job for a mate of the people involved with issuing the tender.

There are still only a very few virtual tours of National Trust properties and none that I know of that were specifically designed for the disabled. This is a disgrace as there are many NT properties that are, in whole or part, difficult or impossible for the disabled to visit, and the Disability and Discrimination Act requires that the disabled are given equal or equivalent access to all sites that the public can visit. In many cases, this can only mean some sort of virtual tour.

Sometime later, we were in contact with the Local Authority that owned Tredegar House, near Newport in South Wales, who wanted a virtual tour for the disabled as the house is on many different levels! We produced a beautiful touch-screen programme, which included portraits in words and pictures of Sir Henry Morgan, the privateer and Governor of Jamaica, who was a member of the family that owned Tredegar House, also the bizarre occultist Aleister Crowley, similarly. If you are an addict of Antiques Roadshow, like me, you will see the approach to Tredegar House, and its lovely gilded iron gates, with the house behind it, at the start of every programme.

Rather, as in the case of Westminster Abbey, Private Eye uncovered a scandal concerning the management of the National Trust. Their Director-General, Fiona Reynolds, moved their Head Office from Queen Anne's Gate, overlooking St. James's Park in Central London, out to Swindon in the early 2000s, overlooking the fact that the NT had recently signed a new 25-year lease on the London premises, with the lease stipulating that the property could not be sub-let.

To compound matters they had taken on another building next door on the same basis. The NT, a body at least partly supported by donations of one kind or another from the general public, had to pay for these leases for the next twenty years, though the buildings remain empty, and it is not as if the NT does not already own considerable numbers of very large buildings all over the country – surely one or other of them would have been suitable. The building at Swindon is typically soulless and modern with no extenuating features, apart from its high cost!

To cap it all, Fiona Reynolds, who was created a Dame, paid herself over £250,000 in relocation expenses to cover the cost of her own move to Swindon, which is conveniently commutable from the Reynolds family home near Cirencester, about twenty miles away. Private Eye informed us that she had already possessed that property for some years, so her moving expenses would have been trivial.

She got the job at the NT from her position as Director of the Women's Unit in Tony Blair's cabinet office, whatever that did. The National Trust is a charity, and its website states, "We depend more than ever on the energy of our volunteers and staff, and we know many of our supporters face all kinds of financial hardship. More than ever, we need to demonstrate that the Trust is time and money well spent. We must make every penny count..." Yeah, right. Charitable organisations seem to attract individuals who take the view that "not-for-profit" does not mean "not for their personal profit".

Ms Reynolds' later fiasco was to spend hard-earned NT cash on re-branding their logo, i.e. making the oak leaves smaller and less hard-edged, removing the "The" from the National Trust name and using upper and lower case letters for "National Trust" as opposed to all upper case letters used hitherto.

Apparently, this exercise cost several hundred thousands of pounds. Great value, obviously, and indicative of the usually futile exercise to align themselves to a new image that organisations which do actually have better things to do, indulge in as displacement activity.

The Great Post Office Swindle – Revealed

Although I had no part in this appalling rip-off, I was there when the plot was originally taking shape and knew some of the people involved. Let's start at the beginning. When I was running the banking and financial sector sales operation at Nixdorf Computer in the mid-1980s I had heard through contacts that the Post Office were looking to automate the counters in their main (Crown) Post Offices throughout the country and that when this had been completed essentially the same system, though with just one (usually) terminal device, would be installed in the local Post Offices run by their network of sub-postmasters. Nixdorf had supplied not dissimilar systems on the Continent of Europe and of course had supplied numerous bank branch systems to the Midland Bank and Anglia Building Society in the UK, for example. One would have expected therefore that the Post Office would make enquiries of Nixdorf, amongst others, as to what they would propose. To my alarm and dismay I then heard that they were only proposing to talk to ICL (as it then was) who had no experience of retail banking, or indeed any other retail systems, and no appropriate hardware nor software. This had all the appearances of a dog's dinner, to use the technical term.

I realised that there was no point in pleading our case on rational commercial or technical terms since the ICL choice was purely a political one – because the company was British. I needed political clout. Fortunately I had met a great friend of my father-in-law – they were both MPs and anti-Common Market, called Sir William (Bill) Clark. He had been Conservative party Treasurer and was a very considerable businessman in his own right. As will be apparent to you by now, I was not a great one for pulling strings, nor any sort of politician, but I realised that even if I never did such a thing again, I had to do it now. So I 'phoned Bill Clark – even I knew enough to keep such things off the written record – explained the position and told him that there was a potential disaster looming which, as the Post Office was a public service, might rebound on the Government. He didn't commit to any action, being the discreet and highly capable individual that he was, but miraculously I was suddenly able to speak to the head of the team reviewing the situation at the Post office. I invited him and his team out to the banking seminar in Brussels mentioned earlier and we got along very well. Not long after, my people became involved in discussions with the PO and we received a considerable order for counter and back-office systems for the main Royal Mail Post Offices. I put my top systems man onto the project and at first it went swimmingly.

At this moment my boss, Mike Hart, realising that this would in due course become a massive order, therefore wanted a direct part in it, together with the resulting commission. He therefore moved me off to develop some interactive video training systems and I lost contact with the PO project and left Nixdorf soon after. By that time Heinz Nixdorf, who I had met, had died and an incompetent called Arno Bohn had taken over. Hart and Bohn were buddies and I would therefore never have been able to reverse Hart's decision so there was no point in trying. I also knew full well that Nixdorf had taken all the wrong technical decisions after their founder's death and that they would be going under very soon; which indeed came about a couple of years afterwards when Siemens took them over.

Before all this happened, I had proposed to the PO that they must include an "audit trail", tamper-proof printer in the configuration for the main post offices, but particularly for the local counters run by sub-postmasters. This was to ensure that whatever the central computer records said, there was a printed proof of every transaction in the local office. This procedure was neither unusual, nor technically difficult, nor a particularly expensive add-on, but it would safeguard the sub-postmasters if a dispute arose since they could produce a printed record of every transaction and a running balance which would validate their till receipts. This is blindingly obvious and was the basic reason why cash registers incorporate such devices so I was horrified when I later learnt through my contacts that this process had been eliminated. (Interestingly I heard recently from a highly reputable source that at least one of the sub-postmasters had been so worried about this aspect that he/she had gone to all the trouble of keeping a running hand-written record of every transaction.) For this omission to happen it was convenient/necessary to take the project away from Nixdorf or ICL (where it had reverted to after Nixdorf's demise) and hand it to a more compliant company, in this case Fujitsu, who had taken over

ICL. Further than this I can only speculate, but I believe this is what happened, since there is plentiful evidence for every aspect of it.

Someone closely involved, possibly a consultant, realised that because the Post Office is in a special position legally in that it can prosecute sub-postmasters without reference to the police or to the Public Prosecution Service, if a facility was built into the system whereby the PO people controlling the network of local post offices through the so-called "Horizon" system, could 'adjust' the balances of the local offices unilaterally – with no printed proof of every transaction at the terminal ends – it could be used to siphon large sums from those offices for which the sub-postmasters were legally responsible. Obviously special program code would need to be developed to provide such a facility, it could not suddenly appear by accident.

If the sub-postmasters objected, the Post Office would be able to prosecute them with a high probability of success – why would a judge or magistrate believe a little sub-postmaster with poor, or non-existent, legal representation and no printed proof of every transaction, rather than the mighty PO, represented by its own powerful in-house teams of lawyers? Obviously this scam could not be used too frequently, with the likely attendant publicity, or it would become apparent that the sub-postmasters were being ripped-off, but it could be used, or even just the threat of it, very effectively, particularly against those sub-postmasters who were more argumentative/aggressive. The PO could always say that they knew nothing about what was going on as their sub-contractor that ran the network, Fujitsu, actually effected the 'balance adjustments'. This was why the PO continually maintained to the sub-postmasters they were prosecuting that they were "the only ones" being taken to court. One of the many lies or prevarications told by everyone in the PO from its chief executive, Paula Vennells, downwards.

However, for such a scam to be worthwhile, the prime necessity is for the financial aspects to be taken care of in advance so that large sums of money are not floating around in the annual accounts, which would be likely to draw the attention of the PO's accountants. It is a sure sign of a scam when this does not happen and nobody in the PO is disputing the fact that no-one (they allege) knows where the huge sums of money – certainly into the £tens of millions – extracted illegally from the sub-postmasters, have disappeared to. Added to this is the fact that no-one at either the Post Office, or Fujitsu, has actually been prosecuted and most of the sub-postmasters have not yet been compensated after many years of trying, and against all the odds, winning repeatedly in Court. Despite Sir Alan Bates', and others', best and heroic efforts, I see no chance of this matter ending satisfactorily. Ultimately the sub-postmasters have very little hope of success against the combined efforts – funded publicly – of the Post Office, the Government, Fujitsu, and the teams of lawyers involved, collectively – *The Pricks*.

Software Development – Small is Beautiful

I have long held the view that small development teams are far more effective than vast squads of coders, principally because once more than two or three people are involved in a project, they necessarily have to spend a significant part of their time communicating what they are doing to the other members of the team.

Human nature being what it is, they will inevitably fail to communicate what they are doing in full, or even completely correctly, and may even, for personal or pride or selfish reasons, deliberately communicate less than the full picture. An exemplar for the concept of small development teams and individuals was that of Gene Amdahl who almost single-handedly created a new operating system for the IBM-compatible mainframe computers that his company produced in the 1970s. In my own experience at Arbat, the multi-user operating system – far superior to anything from DEC – was produced almost entirely by Peter Facey, at least initially.

Similarly, at Apple, the first system for the Apple II was created by Steve Wozniak, and for the Macintosh, it was produced largely by Jef Raskin, with the all-important graphics interface designed and programmed by Bill Atkinson, who also produced Hypercard, Hypercard was the first real hypermedia programme based on Ted Nelson's hypertext work. Linux was created by Linus Torvalds.

We all use hypertext when we link from one page of a website to another by clicking on a link. Its significance was that instead of using IF statements and GOTO commands, which, when nested, are terribly confusing and difficult to debug, the happy programmer could just initiate a jump to another 'card', or webpage.

All the above were supported, often later on in the development, by teams, but those individuals initiated the design and maintained its objectives and consistency. This is in complete contrast to the vast armies of programmers at Microsoft for example, or those working on Government projects in the UK. For the latter especially, the objective is often not to finish the job but rather to ensure that it continues for as long as possible so that they are employed, even if not particularly gainfully.

This usually results in badly designed and inefficient code, which, even when it is tested, is not tested thoroughly, often because the testing throws up so many errors that a re-design is required to make it work at all, and so an endless cycle begins. Frequently, the people who actually know how the task is done in a government department are not involved at all in the design of the programme as it is handed over to an outside contractor who knows little and cares less, just as long as he gets paid, which the government seems happy to do regardless of whether that contractor had completed projects successfully for the government in the past. Roll on the gravy train for Capita, Fujitsu and other major contractors.

The revolution in programming, thanks to more powerful multimedia tools such as MacroMedia Director and Dreamweaver, has meant that, in theory, it is much quicker to produce a programme containing sound, pictures, video, etc., with the aid of them. However, the downside is that though it is faster to produce a demonstration or prototype programme, the bugs and in-built restrictions in those software suites mean that producing a real programme can actually take longer than starting from scratch in a programming language such as 'C++' where the programmer has complete control over the system. The advent of the No code/Low code technology may change this and has been used very successfully in our Falls Database system, for example.

In addition, the programmer working in Director may have to deal with and control other software elements such as QuickTime (to play movies) from within Director, and he will then discover that it is often almost impossible to do so in order to produce the desired effect. For marketing reasons, the publishers/vendors of these programmes rarely, if ever, bother to fix the bugs in the current versions before releasing a new version with new features.

So the net result is that the shiny new software package with such alluring new features will include all the existing bugs, plus some new ones associated with those new features. You can imagine how frustrating this is, especially as you are expected to take the new package in order to maintain compatibility with newer versions of the operating system, etc. and the vendor's support is usually focussed on the new version – which you will often have to have paid more money for, in addition to the original package purchase price.

One result of the enormous increase in processor speed and ready availability at very low cost of massive memory stores, both on disc and on-chip, is that programmers are encouraged to be lazy in the use of resources so that a new version of the operating system will use gigabytes of memory and may take ages to load onto the system.

In fact, the increase in the size and complexity of the OS is running in parallel with the provision of faster chips and more memory so that, in effect, the hardware advances are consumed by the OS, with little or no net benefit to the user. As fast as Intel introduce a new generation of faster chips, Microsoft releases a new version of Windows that sucks up all/much of the increased power.

Combined with the necessity for Windows to be backwards compatible with all its previous versions, this has made it almost impossible to offer real advances in capability to the user. Apple Computer at least had the corporate foresight and willpower to abandon old versions of their hardware and software and gently move their users in stages onto new OS, and indeed new hardware, when they abandoned Motorola and moved to Intel 32-and 64-bit processors. This produced real advances in speed and usability for the user.

It seems unimaginable nowadays that powerful operating systems ran on minicomputers in the 1970s using just 64K or 128K of 16-bit memory, including all the programmes to control dumb terminals, which were swapped in and out from disc by the OS as needed. They also controlled scores of teleprinters and communications links to mainframe computers, as well as monitoring a very large network. In fact they were handling simultaneous input from far more sources and producing much more useful output than is typical of the PCs or Macs of today, which are a million times more powerful.

Nobody nowadays writes or uses re-entrant code, which involved designing routines common to a number of different programmes and which were called as required by those programmes. Re-entrant code was highly efficient in storage and processing terms but is long gone. Have you ever wondered why your new 24GHz PC with 2 Tbytes of RAM takes what seems like forever to load up the operating system and become usable? Well, it is because legions of programmers have been doing their own thing with little regard to anyone else's code, so the duplication of code and function is enormous.

An excellent example of "small is beautiful" is the bet settling system that Arbat produced for Ladbrokes. The core of it was written by a programmer at Arbat who had an inspirational moment while travelling home on the London Underground one evening, wrote the algorithm down on the back of a cigarette packet and tested it out the next morning in the office. The problem was – at the time – that a complex multiple series of doubles and trebles, especially in an eight-horse accumulator called a Gigantic, was incredibly difficult to work out accurately, especially in the fevered atmosphere of a busy betting shop.

So, the task was delegated to Ladbroke's chief bet settler at their Head Office in Harrow. He did not believe it could be done on any computer, large or small, so we challenged him to calculate it himself with a set of winning horses, complicated by last-minute changes where a horse had not started or there had been a dead heat. It took the computer half a second, but the bet settler took three and a half hours and got it wrong!

After that, we were in, so we installed the system in their Credit Betting operation, which paid for itself in under six months. Incidentally, on the first of a series of visits there, they told me that they were really worried because one of their punters was up, first £70,000 and, worse, when I next visited, £150,000 and they were thinking of shutting their entire credit betting operation down as that was all it then earned in an average year.

The punter was a well-known Soho restaurateur and they had closed his account – because he was too successful – on a previous occasion and did not want to do it again because of the bad publicity. Obviously, I was getting nervous too that the whole project was about to go out of the window, but the next time I visited them, they told me all was OK – he now owed them £35,000!

Unfortunately, we could not source the manufacture of terminal systems for the thousands of betting shops who could have benefitted from the system at what was then a low enough cost to make the project viable. Amongst others, we tried Systime, a DEC OEM and terminal manufacturer in Leeds, whose managing director left the crucial meeting with myself and Ladbrokes to take delivery of his new Ferrari – he already had a company helicopter. Ladbrokes' Finance Director retorted that he did not expect to pay for such extravagances, and the meeting broke up soon afterwards.

Systime did, however produce a one-off terminal to Jos Roberts' design, which had some very impressive new features. Jos had built a mock counter to fit around it, but it tended to make the device overheat, so we had to turn it off before the presentation, thus requiring the bootup procedure to be actually carried out during the demonstration, which turned it into a rather drawn-out affair and exposed some of its less than fully thought-out aspects.

Although Ladbrokes did not order the terminals, they were generous enough to insist on paying us for our work, as well as for the Credit Betting system. In fact they were some of the brightest, quickest and easiest people I have ever had to deal with – no wonder they have run rings around the racing authorities for years.

I have long worked with a perfectionist – William Donelson – a computer scientist who learned his trade in the very early stages of the development of personal computers at the Architecture Machine Laboratory, later the Media Lab, at Massachusetts Institute of Technology in the 1970s where he developed the Spatial Data Management System, the first multimedia user interface.

He also worked on the first virtual tour of Aspen, Colorado. Working with a perfectionist is a nightmare if you are a marketing man because he will take immense pains to get the product right rather than out of the door as quickly as possible. However, the net result is that programmes he created many years ago, such as Foul Play, still run without errors, and the support overhead for existing products is virtually zero, so actually, I am extremely grateful to him and do my best to curb my impatience.

It is true to say that William has produced some amazing and ground-breaking programmes, such as Foul Play, Explore Parliament and the Taj Mahal website, which have been imitated, but never surpassed. How many programmes have you ever encountered that you can just walk up to when they are running at a public kiosk and use them without any instruction because the user interface is so intuitive? I would bet that the answer is close to zero.

However this is the norm for William's programmes – I wish I could say the same for anyone else's.

We had an extraordinary experience with Xerox who wanted us to film the **inside** of a new digital printing system that they had launched. The idea was to provide images for their maintenance engineers showing the paper track, rollers, etc., inside the machine, whose cabinets could be separated to reveal its innards.

It was a truly ground-breaking machine as it could take digital images from a variety of sources and complete the entire printing process at very high speed, and so was intended for large stores and supermarkets that needed instant vouchers or some sort of instant promotion of their product. It could even print wallpapers. The first system in Europe was installed in Paris, so we travelled there by Eurostar and, as may be imagined, the lighting and set up was very difficult.

Nevertheless, we managed to produce some high-quality 360° panoramic images and, after processing them, handed them over to our contact at Xerox, who seemed pleased enough – and indeed, we got paid soon after. We were very keen to get a copy of the finished product, which was a CD-ROM with other training material on it, in order to use it as a good reference. However not only did they refuse to give us a copy of the disc, but they would not even show it to us. I imagine that they had some sort of paranoia about competitors copying their design.

Healthcare for the Aged – Falling for a Dream

There are some people who live in a dream world, and there are some who face reality; and then there are those who turn one into the other. Erasmus

After 15 years of virtual travel development and numerous successful, beautiful, informative and innovative programmes to show for it, Armchair Travel suddenly became obsolete when Google launched Google Maps and Streetview in 2007/8. It quickly became apparent that they would cover, if they did not already, every interesting location on land on the planet, as they were using their enormous advertising revenues to create a comprehensive digital map of the world, complete with 360° panoramic images of every conceivable location – and delivering it online for free, by using their advertising revenues to cover the cost.

There was clearly no way that my company could compete, so William and I licked our wounds, folded our tents and closed Armchair Travel for any future business. Sad, but there was no point in dragging out the agony. All our competitors, except Google, did the same. The real pity was that we had had a contact with Nokia to produce virtual tours of 100 cities, with assistance from Insight Guides, who were supposed to provide local information on them.

We had the idea long before Google even existed, just as I had had the idea for an Amazon-type business and proposed it to the head of one of the most iconic stores in London – the General

Trading Company in Sloane Street – in the 1970s, twenty years before Bezos came along – indeed he was only twelve years old at the time!

So, what to do? My friend, Jeremy Westwood, CEO of Insight Guides, had said to me, "Never retire, William. Doing so was the greatest mistake of my life". Sadly, he died a couple of years later. But how was I to occupy my time, let alone make a living? Two events changed my life. First, my sister-in-law suffered the second of two broken hips in a fall at home, the previous one having happened several years before.

My wife, Virginia, and I visited her in the hospital and were told that she had osteoporosis, making her vulnerable to fractures, and would have to have some weeks of rehabilitation after her two or three weeks in the hospital following her major hip repair operation. I thought that it was unacceptable that someone who was clearly at risk of a second fall and fracture was left completely unprotected.

Indeed, on researching the matter, I found that 50% of those who fractured one hip fall again and fracture the other and that no less than 3 million people in the UK have the disease. Why was nothing being done about this? I then looked at the various approaches that had been taken and quickly realised that nobody in their right mind would wear any of the protective devices then available, and clearly, there was no way of remedying, nor even slowing – certainly at that time, and probably still pertaining now – the progression of osteoporosis, which, relating generally to a lack of oestrogen after the menopause, affects mainly women. Osteoporosis means the bones become porous and liable to fracture in a fall.

So, what to do about the problem? Fortunately, I saw at that time in 2009 in the newspaper a report of a new wonder material that had been developed at Hatfield University, which absorbed impacts very effectively and was being used by the winter sports fraternity. The company had the curious name of D3O and was based down in Brighton. I contacted them, proposing that I use their material to make hip protectors, which would be both more comfortable and more effective in absorbing impact forces than anything else currently available. They were somewhat sceptical at first but warmed to the idea when I agreed in principle that we would pay them a licence fee for the technology, provided that the company I was setting up had the exclusive use of their technology for medical purposes.

The next problem was to get finance for the project as we would clearly have to pay a substantial amount for a supply of stock, as well as covering the licence fee, in order to commence business. I approached some old friends, Lavinia and David Aykroyd, and through David (helped by my half-nephew Danny Beckett) Crispin Odey, the founder of the then-leading hedge fund company. They sounded interested so I then arranged a visit for myself, David and Lavinia to D3O in Brighton.

D3O was at that time crammed into a small one-room office, with a laboratory next door, in a rented-out building near the railway station there. We were met by the founder of the company, Richard Palmer, who was a keen snowboarding enthusiast, which had led him to seek a way of protecting himself from injury in the horrendous 15-foot+ falls encountered from the edge of a run in an icy, concrete half-pipe. Up to that time, the standard protection was a hard plastic shell with interior padding, which constricted the movement and was both uncomfortable and not very effective in absorbing impacts. Encouragingly, the parts that needed to be protected, such as the hands, elbows, shoulders, and knees, also included the hips, so the company had developed pads that fitted into the special clothing worn for such sports.

D3O had had recent great success at the 2010 Vancouver Olympics, where the USA and Canadian ski teams wore 'Spider' suits with pads on their forearms and thighs for the Giant Slalom and Super G events, where it is vital to ski as close as possible to the gates in order to shave milliseconds off the run time. Conversely, the suits needed to be as aerodynamic and tight-fitting as possible, which invalidated bulky padding material.

Impacting even spring-loaded gates at 70+ mph, causes severe bruising and tended to make the skiers not ski as aggressively as was necessary to podium in the event. Gratifyingly, the USA and

Canadian teams and individuals, mens' and womens', won both events at the Games, establishing the D3O company in that sport.

D3O had also had success in meeting the requirements of the motorcycling fraternity for padding incorporated into the mandatory leather clothing to protect riders in a fall as their material was thinner, more flexible and more effective than any other. Amusingly, Richard Palmer demonstrated the efficacy of the material by producing a shovel and hitting himself hard on the knee! He explained that he had previously been in the habit of hitting his head with it, but it did tend to make him a bit dizzy.

Why was D3O so effective? He explained that it was a composite material that he and a colleague had invented/developed at Hatfield University several years before. It was a polyurethane with about 3% of a dilatant that caused the molecules to lock together instantly (within 1 millisecond) on impact, just as when you do a belly-flop into a pool, it hurts because the water molecules lock on impact. Normally, this phenomenon is confined to liquids, which would not be appropriate for clothing, but the two guys had come up with a process that enabled the material, uniquely, to be delivered in solid form. Obviously, the company had protected it with patents in all significant countries, though at considerable expense.

We all agreed that an exclusive licence for this material for medical purposes seemed like a good idea as I had read that consistently there were about 90,000 hip fractures from falls each year in the UK and three or four times that number in the USA, which would be the key market, especially as D3O revealed that they had had an enquiry from an individual who lived in Washington State, just over the border from Vancouver and he wanted a licence to set up a distribution company for hip protection. Obviously, D3O would not divulge his name or details until we signed a contract with them.

At about this time, I happened to see an episode of Dragons' Den, which featured a company that had licensed the material from D3O to make a protective cover for mobiles. They demonstrated it by starting up a Youtube video on a mobile and then throwing it out of a first-floor window onto a car park. The guy below picked it up and showed the video still running. They got the investment from Dragons' Den.

I formed the company as Hip Impact Protection Limited, or HIP, which, surprisingly, had not been taken up as a name already, and developed a logo, which, if you look at the white space in the centre, shows the body  outline of a woman. Older readers will recall the hourglass-shaped Coca-Cola bottle. Much to my surprise, almost no one notices this.

I also started the process of trademarking the "Fall-Safe" name in as many countries as seemed appropriate. Funnily enough, I discovered that almost no one remarks on the similarity with "fail-safe". Perhaps I shouldn't care, but it always seems a pity after all the thought and work I put into this.

It all now looked like a promising prospect, but I was then confronted by a voluminous 25-page licensing contract from D3O, plus an exhaustive Terms and Conditions agreement. The option of having a lawyer crawl all over it was simply not feasible nor affordable, so I picked out what are always the key clauses concerning rights, payment schedule and termination and checked – with myself and my previous experience with numerous other contracts – to see if they were acceptable!

Though not very favourable, as you would expect, they did not contain any nasty boobytraps, so I signed, having secured the investment needed from the above-mentioned friends. The contract mandated that any licence contract I signed with a distributor would mirror the D3O contract, so D3O, having divulged his name and details, I contacted the man on the West Coast and sent him the proposed contract.

Nothing came back to me until the last day before the deadline I had set. I had more or less given up and so went off to watch the Test Match at Lords, where I got a call from my wife to say that the contract had been returned by fax from their lawyers with a list of amendments a mile long. I immediately returned to my office in our flat in South Kensington and set about working through the contract.

As the deadline was looming up the next day, there was no alternative but to work through the night to sort it out – and I suspect that their lawyers had anticipated that I would have to submit it to my lawyers, with concomitant delay, and thus miss the deadline. I went through all their proposed amendments, and there were several on each page, and responded at 4 am the following day with a document that met all their requirements, without compromising any of mine. They really had no alternative but to sign it the next day.

So, after months of preparation, we were all set to go with a contract with D3O and one with the distributor, which had sufficient volumes of product to cover the licence fee and make a profit.

I ordered and paid for the mandated minimum volumes of product from D3O, and they had offered to supply either from a manufacturer in China or from a polyurethane moulding company in Kent that they recommended and had used successfully before. I quizzed them about this, and they said that either company would produce a very acceptable product, so I opted for the UK manufacturer on the basis that I would have more control of the process and that the shipment costs would be lower, and delivery more speedy.

I went through a design process for the product with the D3O people and opted for an approach that included about 20 air holes and clever ducting on the inside of the pad to allow air to pass through and keep the skin cool underneath the pad. About two months later, I received the first 20 production samples from D3O. I immediately responded by saying that I thought most of them were unacceptable as they contained many small craters on their surfaces as a result of bubbling during the production process.

My problem with this is that in a hospital environment, products must be kept clean and, if possible, sterile so that bacteria or viruses do not proliferate. Clearly, pads with numerous small cell holes all over both sides could harbour such germs and thus endanger the patient. D3O had not encountered this problem before as all their products had previously been provided sewn-in to clothing of one sort or another. I did not wish to sew the pads into underpants, for example, as the Americans were going to use their own pants supplier for cost and convenience reasons.

Also, I wanted to be able to supply UK customers with a pack containing 3 or 4 pairs of pants and a single pair of pads since that would be much cheaper than our competitors, who generally supplied 3 sets of pants each with pads sewn-in, obviously at much greater cost. The point was that the bare pads would be only too visible to the hospital or care home nurses, who would probably reject them for the cavities.

As several of the pads only demonstrated this adverse effect to a minimal degree, I foolishly accepted D3O's assurances that they would be the norm and that the others were just a temporary, pre-production aberration. So, with some misgivings, I OKayed the samples, and the moulding facility went ahead with production, albeit much more slowly than I had been assured would be the case.

Eventually, they were ready to deliver, and as I did not then have any warehouse facilities in London or elsewhere and was forbidden by D3O to visit the moulding factory, I arranged for the delivery to go directly to the States. Big mistake: always check the product quality before delivery to a customer.

As it happened, the new CEO of the US distributors was visiting the UK at the same time as the delivery took place. I met him, and he was very upset, to say the least, as he had just heard that his colleagues in the US had inspected the goods and were very unhappy with them. I had arranged for him to visit D3O's new offices in Hove and meet their people. It was not a friendly meeting.

D3O claimed, incorrectly as it later turned out, that the bubbling was endemic to the production process. They had more difficulty explaining away the dirt embedded in much of the product and the 'flashing' covering many of the air circulation holes.

It was agreed that the entire shipment would be returned to the UK for inspection – at D3O's expense. Virginia and I went down to Hove to check it all out, box by box – some 20,000 pieces. It turned out that about 16% of the product was unacceptable for dirt, bubbling and/or flashing. This is way more than anyone would expect from a production process, assuming that the product had been inspected at all before it left the factory. So, before they restarted production to make up the deficit, I requested that they let me inspect the factory.

D3O refused, as it might compromise the integrity of their "secret" process of manufacturing and, thereby, their patents. They would, however, allow a consultant to visit the factory under a confidentiality agreement and produce a report – at my expense. His report noted that it was the dirtiest factory he had ever encountered, amongst other criticisms.

Obviously it is not acceptable for medical devices, such as Fall-Safe, to exhibit even small black marks on them. I demanded that in future, there would be much less bubbling and no dirty marks or flashing, or I would reject the whole shipment. So, the factory made up the 16% difference with new product, and we shipped the whole lot to the USA at D3O's expense. The problem was that this whole nightmare had taken about five months to resolve, had infuriated me and my distributors, and lost a key investor in the USA who was going to partner with the distributor but who unfortunately, and sadly, died in the meantime.

Amazingly, the new CEO of D3O had the nerve to tell me that I "had accused all his senior executives of lying", so I said, "If the cap fits…", actually I had done no such thing, which rather proves my point, at least in his case.

The CEO of the US distributors flew to Florida for the annual jamboree, sorry conference, of the Dept. of Veterans Affairs, which is the key provider of care for retired members of the US armed forces, with around 500 hospitals. Though he had been a doctor in the Royal Navy, he managed to get DVT in one leg on the return flight to Seattle and nearly died, which set back the marketing of the product in the USA more than somewhat; though when he did eventually recover, he was not surprisingly, more interested in progressing the highly successful lavender business he was building up, and which centred on his farm there.

However, a pair of Dutch guys had contacted me and wanted to have our product tested at the labs of the University of Amsterdam and compared with all the other hip protector products on the market in Europe. They had been in the hip protector business for some time but had had problems with a product that did not work well and allowed some people to break their hip in a fall, so they wanted something better. I sent them a sample, and the test results obtained on Amsterdam University's test rig that they sent it to be checked out on, triumphantly vindicated my product.

He then signed a contract under which we delivered a substantial number of products each month. He could not keep to that so we reverted to a significant delivery every 2-3 months. They were likeable guys, but rogues really as although they did not let us down and paid their bills promptly, he had not paid his taxes, so suddenly had to take off with his company to Bulgaria! I visited him a couple of times while he was still in Utrecht, flying from City Airport to Rotterdam. On one of them, the pilot announced that though there was fog at Rotterdam, he had enough fuel onboard to allow him to fly round the airport a couple of times. We all wondered what would happen if twice was not enough!

After abandoning D3O and their useless manufacturer, I got the product produced by a brilliant company in China (without infringing D3O's patents) and put it up on Amazon, Fall-Safe being the first hip protectors to be sold on that platform. We also signed up distributors in France, Ireland, Australia and in Scandinavia. Two very nice Italians were very keen to distribute it in Italy, and they invested in a stand at an exhibition in Siena which went down very well, but then they told me that the average payment delay in Italy was 354 days! They also introduced me to a company which had developed a wristband device that improved your balance.

You tested it by standing side-by-side with someone and, with both of you with arms locked straight down, you cupped their fist in your hand, and you lifted. Without the wristband, it was easy to lift the other person, so they overbalanced, but if they were wearing it, it was impossible! This device was used by professional archers and cyclists in Italy to improve their balance and had been tested in various labs in Italy and Madrid with good results.

The active element in it was at the far end of the infra-red spectrum. I thought this would complement our line of products, but was chary of providing it to the public, other than at cost price to friends – at their own risk – because there might have been some unknown side effects. Eventually, the Italian company went bust. I intend to revive it when opportunity arises and when it is possible to monitor people for falls, which leads to the next product.

In about 2011, I attended a conference on falls in London at which a senior nurse gave a talk and stated that most falls were not recorded, or even observed, if no injury resulted because either no one was about or the faller had dementia and simply did not remember that they had had a fall, or they were picked up from the floor by a fellow resident/patient, or by a non-nursing member of staff, who did not record it. She mentioned that at home, people who fell usually did not tell anyone either because they forgot to/did not think it important, if no injury resulted, or because they were afraid that if they did so, it might result in them being admitted to a care home.

The nurse mentioned that the first serious fall sometimes resulted in a broken wrist as the person put out a hand to protect themselves, so the next time, they did not do that, and if it was a sideways fall, they broke their hip. There is a natural aversion to falling on your face, so fallers falling forward tend to twist to one side during the fall. Recording a fall with the use of CCTV cameras was not welcomed because nobody wants a camera in a bedroom or bathroom, where about 40% of all falls occur.

It is also the case that it can easily take an hour of a nurse's time to fill in the forms recording a fall. How many times do you want to do that in a day? Given that there are about half a million falls that result in an injury every year in the UK, this is a serious problem, costing the NHS around £4.5 billion a year, every year and mounting as the population ages and emergency services and hospital facilities become more and more over-stretched, and expensive.

Another problem is that 50% of those who have fallen suffer thereafter from a pronounced "fear of falling", which itself can lead to more falls, as we can see on the ski slopes. Last but not least, around 30% of those who do fracture a hip die within a year from complications.

What have the NHS, NICE and co. done to combat the menace of falls? First, they came up with "multifactorial interventions", which include a variety of nostrums, e.g. bed bars and special mats, that were subsequently proved not to have any impact on the number of falls and fractures in a large-scale (46,000 patient) clinical trial in Australia.

Amazingly, the Royal College of Physicians adopted this approach and had the nerve to call it 'Fall-Safe', exactly as per our hip protector product, but when they tried it, they found that it actually **increased** the number of falls by 14%! The NHS then tried balance exercises and trained 400 physiotherapists, or the like, to administer them across the country. Unfortunately, they were unable to get the elderly to perform these exercises once the trainer had moved on to the next healthcare facility, and even when they did manage to make them persist with the exercises, they found that the unsupervised exercises increased the number of falls.

The earlier attempts at providing hip protectors focussed primarily on the use of a hard polyethylene shell, which stopped the Greater Trochanter breaking off at the neck – the usual type of fracture – but transferred the impact force to the thigh/femur, which caused, in some cases, a fracture of the pelvis.

This gave hip protectors a bad name from about the year 2005 onwards and had two other effects. First, NICE and the Cochrane Review (a well-regarded source of medical device information) responded by not advocating the use of hip protectors, except in special circumstances and for facilities that had 24-hour supervised nursing – presumably to ensure that the patients/residents were actually wearing them. They also noted that pelvic fractures sometimes occurred when wearing these devices. Second, most of the hip protector manufacturers dumped the hard shell products and produced soft padding products using a shell with a soft foam pad on the body side, airbags with a foam insert, or textile pads.

These, to say the least, were not particularly effective in preventing fractures. However, despite the arrival on the scene of my product in 2011, which was able to absorb 70% of the impact and still be thinner and softer, cooler and more comfortable than any other, neither NICE nor Cochrane was inclined, and still aren't, to update their recommendations, which date from 2004. Shame on them.

Clearly, as a late entrant into an established market, we needed to establish our credibility by demonstrating that our product worked better than anyone else's. D3O had a test rig that dropped a weight half a metre onto a metal dome, simulating a hip joint, but it was primarily geared for showing that they met the relevant ISO standard for motorcycle gear, which is a completely different kind of fall from an elderly person's. By chance, I met Professor Julian Minns, who was, and still is, the pre-eminent world expert on hip protector testing, amongst other claims to fame.

Fortunately, he already had a test rig, and I visited him, and we performed a series of tests using it in his garage. To my delight, they showed that our pads absorbed about 70% of the impact of a fall, which is sufficient to prevent all hip fractures. We also tested pads from our main UK, European and US competitors, and they all showed much less impact absorption capability than ours.

However, life is never that simple, and I learnt from Julian that there was soon to be a conference at the British Standards Institution

(BSI) because it had been proposed that a new standard should be instituted for hip protectors.

Naturally, I asked permission to attend, along with several of our competitors in the UK, including a Danish manufacturer called Tytex, which produced a pad made from textiles – which Julian and I had tested and shown to perform worse than any of the others. I was rather concerned when, after the meeting, a group of people, including a couple of professors, went into a huddle and conversed quietly amongst themselves. What was going on? Well, I soon found out from Julian that they were going to propose a test rig set-up that included a giant titanium spring which simulated the supposed tendency of the human body to "bounce" on impact with the floor/ground.

Needless to say, there was no evidence that this actually occurred, but it did mean that the Tytex pad performed much better than any other, and Dr Stephen Robinovitch (SR) from the University of British Columbia had built a test rig to demonstrate this, complete with spring. The 'good' doctor was a paid consultant to Tytex, so he had a point to prove.

Interestingly, he had obtained his PhD from MIT for advocating a technology that was basically similar to ours, except that his proposed design was a liquid, which became a solid on impact. Just how practical it would have been to carry around a bag of liquid on each hip was not explained in his thesis! No mention in it was made of the body bouncing on contact with the floor. There was also a major logical error in his paper. Clearly, he should never have been awarded a PhD for it.

I was more than somewhat dismayed by this turn of events as it became increasingly clear that SR, aided by a doctor at Imperial College and a Welsh colleague from a test lab in Cardiff, were determined to get the spring included in the proposed BSI standard. A year or so later the BSI called a meeting at their HQ in West London, to which all interested parties were invited. Naturally SR was to attend, having travelled all the way from Vancouver for it, along with a woman who was the director of Tytex, coming from Denmark.

However, they did not know that I had prepared a couple of surprises for them. First, I had loaned the test rig that Julian had had built for me (identical to his own) to a test lab company called Intertek and asked them to use it to test our product. Not coincidentally, Intertek had been proposed by the spring-loaded group as the location for a test facility.

Fortunately, I managed to get a report from them verifying that they had used a non-spring, or normal test rig (mine) and that it was satisfactory in every respect and that our product performed to a satisfactory standard. This was a bombshell at the meeting. Secondly, I had managed to get a friend, who owned a sports facility testing company to test our product, which he did with satisfactory results, who was also to attend the meeting. Third, I had read a paper that SR and others had submitted to Osteoporosis International (OI), a noted scientific publication on the subject, and the article stated unequivocally that the presence of osteoporosis in the faller did *not* make a fracture of the hip more likely in a fall.

All the evidence from decades of research contradicts that assertion. When one of the professors claimed that a paper published in OI had endorsed the use of a spring, I was able to retort that a). SR, already compromised by his paid consultancy work with Tytex, and his pals at BC University, had written that paper, and b). that OI had no credibility if they thought osteoporosis was not a factor in hip fracture. I also mentioned the error in SR's thesis, so he retorted that "He (Beckett) is the elephant in the room"! Some time later I met him again at a conference, a so-called "Falls Festival", in Bologna and went up to him in the huge conference room and asked him why he was now choosing to be in the same room as an elephant! I got no reply.

The meeting broke up in disarray, and after several very unpleasant, indeed libellous, emails from SR, I was able to get the proposed standard kicked into the long grass. SR did not entirely give up because several years later, he managed to get the Canadian standards authority to endorse his spring testing approach for hip protectors.

Fortunately, it does not seem to have had much effect, except possibly in Canada. The data on falls that I hope to obtain from Fall-Safe Assist, see below, should comprehensively prove that our hip protectors prevent 100% of all hip fractures, making such standards obsolete.

Interestingly, the same Canadian university ran a one-year trial in 14 care homes, with 1,000 participants, a couple of years ago, using video cameras in public areas to record all passers-by, thereby capturing a number of falls (at the expense of people looking through thousands of hours of video footage). They found that the wearing of (Tytex and one other type of) hip protectors prevented 64% of all hip fractures. This corresponded to the fact that they were only worn 60% of the time. It also found that no less than 16 fallers had broken a hip whilst wearing thr Tytex (or one other) hip protectors.

The reason that hip protectors are typically not 100% effective in preventing all fractures, regardless of their specific performance in a particular fall, is that they are generally not worn in the two most dangerous environments in the home, or indeed care home, as regards falls – for it has been well researched that more than 40% of all falls occur in the bathroom or bedroom. The reasons for this are obvious when you look at the necessity for wearing pants with side pockets to hold hip protectors in place.

These pants tend to make the device too hot and uncomfortable to wear in bed at night, so they are usually discarded with other outer clothing for the night, and in the bathroom, they obviously cannot be worn in bath, shower or when on the loo. Drowsiness, poor lighting at night, wet, slippery floors, etc., all may play their part in increasing the likelihood of a fall in those locations.

I determined to do something about this because, after all, who would want a remedy that only worked part of the time? At a conference and exhibition in the Royal Geographical Society, where I gave a presentation on hip protectors, I met a lady, Maggi Tebrake, from 3M, at their stand. In a rare moment of inspiration, I asked her if 3M could provide an adhesive film that would stick the pad to a person's hip.

She said, "of course", they already provided adhesives for wound dressings, which were an equally sensitive application, to elderly people with 'thin skin'. So began a long period of testing various solutions from 3M until we got it right and produced a conjunction of pad surface and film that stayed firmly in place, but (the film) could be peeled off from the pad after a fortnight since the skin renews itself after about 15 days and it is not a good idea to have skin residue hanging around.

On the body side of the film, the silicone adhesive is the same as that used in wound dressings and holds the pad firmly, but gently, in place for a fortnight, though it allows the pad to be removed to inspect the skin underneath several times during that period, and replaced. Bingo! However, it took several years before I could convince the Department of Veterans Affairs in the US and some large hospitals in Hong Kong that this was a great idea. A side benefit was that we no longer needed to supply pants in different sizes. We called the device "Fall-Safe Apply". It is unique in that it enables the pads to be worn in the bath and shower and when going to the loo, as well as in bed, comfortably.

So, what to do to verify that falls had occurred? Clearly, something was needed that automatically recorded every fall passed on an alarm message to a central desk in a care home or to the emergency services if the faller was at home. Alarm call devices did indeed exist, and my 90-year-old mother had one, for instance, but she was not wearing it around her neck when she fell on her way to the bathroom in the middle of the night and consequently lay there in the cold for many hours, until a neighbour called in the morning.

Up to that point, she had been relatively fit and well, but the event was the final straw, and she died some weeks later. My sister-in-law fell in similar circumstances but could not get at her alarm pendant, as it was under her clothing. Interestingly, she later fell on some flagstones outside her house but was wearing her hip protector pads and did not suffer a fracture other than some bruises to her arms and legs. The alarm device needed to be unobtrusive since many people we asked in care homes did not like wearing them round their necks as it indicated that they were disabled.

It also needed to be able to register each and every fall automatically because pendants swinging around the neck tended to produce many false positive alarms for every actual fall. Our solution was to embed the pendant in the hip protector pad, which had the advantage of being on the most stable part of the body, so it was possible to re-programme it so that it did not generate any false alarms. I immediately set about patenting this idea, and we quickly obtained a full patent for it in the UK, though a less comprehensive one in the USA and Europe, since their patent offices are oriented towards big business, e.g. Apple, Microsoft, etc. However, these patents would be enough to dissuade any competitors from applying for a similar patent.

The unique selling idea was that the device, which we called Fall-Safe Assist, would protect the faller from a hip fracture and call the emergency services in the event of a fall. Furthermore, we had it programmed to identify the direction of the fall and speed of descent to give the force of the fall when combined with the faller's weight, as those qualities were important when we uploaded the data on every fall to a fall database. Such a database had never been produced hitherto because fall data generated by other devices was not reliable enough to be worth recording. The database meant that we could analyse every fall and collate the information to identify predictors of falls. These predictors might then be used by carers/nurses to introduce actions that might reduce the number of falls in future. This had never been done before.

Alternative approaches were wristwatch devices from Apple and others, though these suffered from a similar rate of false alarms as pendants, since the arms waved about, could mean anything. Also, several companies produced airbags that were held in a belt around the waist and which exploded, literally, into life if a fall was detected. They suffered from numerous disadvantages, such as high cost, but also they tended to tip the faller onto his/her head in a fall, they only recognised about 75% of all falls, if they went off accidentally they could actually cause a fall, and so on. A totally idiotic product, and they have not achieved any market acceptance despite wasting many £millions of investors' money.

I initially went to a company in Massachusetts that promised to deliver a pendant product that was programmed to work from the hip and I paid them for the work to do so. It later turned out that, though they had delivered 25 samples to me, they had not actually done any re-programming, so the device did not work from the hip. Under threat of litigation, they gave in and recompensed me. However, they did also recommend an Israeli company who were, when sufficiently lubricated with money, able to produce a product to our specification.

We continually hear the NHS wingeing that they don't have sufficient budget, despite their spending being similar to the EU average, and when I went to the head of one of the Clinical Commissioning Groups, now superseded by so-called Integrated Care Systems, and pointed out that an average CCG was spending £4.5 million a year on hip fracture repair operations and rehabilitation, which could be radically reduced if hip protectors were supplied, as a preventative measure, to a few thousand of their most frequent fallers, at a initial cost of less than £500,000, they complained that they didn't have £half a million to spend on this.

One wonders where, if anywhere, they get their accountants from. The problem with the NHS is not cash but stupidity or blind bureaucracy, if you prefer it, in an organisation (if that is the right word) employing 1.2 million people. After all, the NHS were quite happy to waste £20 billion on Tony Blair's mad patient record scheme – which had absolutely no chance of ever working – without a single protest. Or look at the damage that the Private Finance Initiative, expanded enormously by Blair and Brown, has done to the hospital building budget. As Einstein said, "The only two things that are infinite are human stupidity and the universe, and I am not sure about the universe".

So, where have we got to with this Fall-Safe Assist project? Well, it is all working and we can show that a genuine fall, and only a genuine fall, is recorded and its characteristics transmitted to the falls database, as well as the emergency services. To put this into effect we applied successfully two years ago to Innovate UK for a grant to complete the falls database.

Our partner, Twin Technology, introduced an expert in Low code/No code technology to me, and he played a blinder in completing the project on time and within budget in the Spring of last year. Perhaps I should not have been surprised that because the initial payment from IUK arrived two months late, and the cut-off end date was 1st April, so what had been proposed as a 6-month project had to be completed in three months. The next step in my policy of continuous product development is to start using AI on the vast amounts of data that the falls sensors will record on the database.

HIP are, therefore, the only company in the world with such technology, and one for which we have a patent, and one would like to think that people are beating a path to our door, given the $50bn that Medicare spends in the US on falls and fractures, but dream on… I am currently trying to get funding for a major trial in UK care homes, which will prove my concept, though a major 3-month trial in Hong Kong last year with 830 patients yielded very high levels of satisfaction from both patients and staff (>70%) – and zero fractures. A similar result was achieved at the Department of Veterans Affairs in the Eastern states of the USA. The VA is perhaps the largest healthcare organisation in the world.

It may be thought that spending 14 years, but less than £1m (which is small change for a major new medical technology) on a project that has still not reached its full potential is an excessive risk to take, but I met another medical device entrepreneur at a conference seven or eight years ago who had given a great presentation about his product, which had become a runaway success, telling us that the next slide would show all the help that NICE and the NHS had given him. It was a blank slide! Anyway he said that they had not made a profit for their first 15 years in the business, so I have about a year to go to emulate him.

In parallel with these developments, just before lockdown, Thady Lillingston, my daughter Serena's eldest son, aged 11, developed a card game with several of his friends and drew it out on a pack of blank playing cards. The whole family played it at Christmas 2019, and we all enjoyed it very much, although some of the cards were difficult to decipher because of their immature drawings. I thought that it was worth producing as a proper card game with professionally drawn cards and advertised for a graphics artist on People Per Hour, a website I had often used very successfully for ad-hoc jobs like website re-design, etc.

By far, the outstanding respondent was a lovely lady in Chandigarh, India, called Param Kaur, who was a teacher with several children of her own and could do the job, for which there was no great hurry, in her spare time (when she had any!) I duly scanned and transmitted the images of Thady's cards to her with explanations, and we began a three-month project. She was delightful to work with – we exchanged over 300 messages over the cards – and she even refused extra payments when one or more of the cards had to be re-drawn through errors on my part.

However, she contacted me some 6 months after we had finished the project and produced the card packs and was clearly in a desperate state as she had been diagnosed with cancer of the womb, I believe, but could not afford the operation. She did not ask for a specific amount of money – as is normal if it is a scam – so I sent her as much as I could afford to borrow, and she duly had the operation, which was a success, and she has gone on to produce many other projects, not least the cartoons in this book, and several games! What would you do in a similar situation?

Later, her husband got Covid while she was still recovering and could not work, so they and their three children were going to be thrown out of their flat for rent arrears. I helped her again, as you would, I hope. Of course, there was a chance that she had taken me for a sucker, but I set that against the certainty that if I was mean and didn't help, and she **was** telling the truth, then her death would be on my conscience forever. The sums of money, though not insignificant, were not a matter of life and death for me.

I contracted her to draw the cartoons in this book, and we came to an arrangement whereby she repaid her borrowings from me by not charging for 2/3rds of the cartoons, so we wound up square after all and are the best of friends.

Incidentally, my wonderful wife, Virginia, and I were staying with some friends many years ago in the country in Devon, and the neighbours, a married couple, were invited over for a drink. It happened that she was the daughter of Mr Dupont, the then richest man in the world, and somehow we got to discuss how mean people were. Virginia, who had not been briefed about them, said, "Well, I have always found that the richest people are the meanest!" Stunned silence while we all hoped the earth would swallow us up, until the Dupont woman said, "Yes, you are so right, honey, that's why they are so rich". Can you imagine Musk or Bezos coming up with that response?

Funding – Apply... or Die!?

Have you ever applied for a grant from some scheme to support small business or innovation? Chances are that you have and that you have been disappointed. Years ago, there was a government grant that companies like Arbat, whose headquarters were in the UK, could apply for to develop new high-tech products.

Enthusiastically, I filled in all the forms, which were pretty voluminous, and sent them all to the Department of Trade and Industry, as it then was. I had applied for a grant to help us develop a message-switching system based on Digital Equipment Corporation mini-computers. There were already a number of message switches on the market and available in the UK, but they all relied on specialist hardware and were foreign-made and imported to the UK by various distributors. We wanted to develop the message-switch using our own much more flexible software and sell it to banks, large companies and organisations like the police and BBC in the UK and then, when we had established a market, launch them abroad.

My proposal was turned down flat by the DTI, and naturally, very disappointed, I retired hurt to lick my wounds. In fact, there was absolutely no discussion with the department, so I got no feedback or even indications why it had not been accepted, though it appeared to meet their criteria at the time. Undeterred, I went on the develop the product, and we sold a system that was more a telex handling system to the Midland Bank, but I had insisted that it be able to cater for the fixed lines to teleprinters, terminals, distributed printers, etc. so that the same software could be used whatever the mix of lines it was connected to.

After the system was installed at the Midland and could therefore be demonstrated to other banks, I sold it to a number of them, and whilst waiting for it to be installed with them, I remembered the grant that we had applied for, dug out the original proposal and re-submitted it, since the criteria for approval now seemed to be the same as before.

To my astonishment I heard a few days later that it had been accepted and that the DTI would be making a grant to us of £50,000. It was a complete mystery to me why we had been turned down a couple of years earlier – when we really needed the money to develop the message switch – yet accepted on identical terms later on when we actually did not need the money for development – as we had already developed the system! Naturally, I did not object or refuse the money because I reckoned they owed us from the previous proposal.

I am sure that this must have happened a great many times to a great many companies, but it is absurd that the grant, which was intended to foster new developments, should have been refused when it was really needed and would have helped enormously, but granted when the development had been completed and, to be honest, was not really needed. I suspect that the DTI felt it was too risky to make a grant initially but felt more confident when Arbat had more of a track record later on, even though this was not the point of making the grant. But having refused it once, they should have been more consistent and refused it again if only on the basis that this was public money and the development in question was not only complete but actually installed and working!

I have since applied for many grants, but it is apparent that the criteria have been drawn more and more tightly, and it is typically extremely difficult to meet them unless your company happens to be a not-for-profit organisation. Armchair Travel has several times been a not-for-profit organisation, though that was not actually what we intended!

However, there is a serious and definite need to provide such grants to small businesses in the UK to enable them to grow and take on staff and mix it with the transatlantic corporations that have easy access to venture capital from business angels who are familiar with high-tech start-ups or early-stage funding. Plenty of people, such as 3i, are happy to provide funding – often for a disproportionate share of the business – when the company is up and running and has secured major orders from big customers – but rarely are they interested in helping to develop new ideas and products.

Before Brexit, I did a lot of research on the then Horizon 2020 funding, particularly in the area of healthcare and medical devices, and was greeted by the statement on their website that "None of these projects have yet reached the market, though we expect some to do so in the near future. In other words, they had, up to that moment, spent over €half a billion on 500 or so healthcare projects that had yielded precisely nothing.

It was interesting that most, if not all, of the funds were given to large companies allied to research institutions, eg teaching hospitals. Clearly, they were using the projects to fund their PhD students. This was confirmed when I attended a funding conference at University College Hospital, co-hosted by UCL, and they told us that their success rate with Horizon 2020 was about 50%, but invariably, they had usually proposed the project to the Horizon organisers in the first place and got them to request offers to meet the specified requirement!

Dragons' Den is a stand-out example of funding anomalies. Obviously, there are many absurd ideas proposed to them, and not infrequently, the presenters of the business propositions are overawed by the occasion or incapable of putting forward their ideas cogently and effectively – that being part of the TV humiliation format. To bad-mouth some of the pioneers standing before them for their failures is uncharitable, and it is noticeable that very few, if any, of the dragons have actually developed and launched entirely **new** inventions themselves. That is far too difficult and risky; much better to piggyback on the efforts of others by taking over their company, or at least a significant share in it, and swiping 40-50% of the profits for comparatively little effort. Or better still, engage in distribution of mobiles or the like, or running companies in the retail and leisure sectors, or on social media.

One might question how much effort the dragons are putting into yet more small investments since they all have their own companies to run, in addition to the ragbag of outfits they have already invested in. What sort of entrepreneur finds it necessary to appear in TV advertisements, as did Peter Jones, wheeling a supermarket trolley around some years ago? Has he not got enough money, or does he just like appearing on TV, however stupid the reason? It was voted the worst celebrity advert of the year by readers of The Sun newspaper.

Yes, certainly, some of the less well-thought-out ideas are wasting everyone's time, but the weeding-out process – which I know personally does go on – should have disposed of them long before they got on primetime TV. Clearly, the producers know this and are only including them for the same reason that obviously untalented performers are included in other "reality TV" talent programmes.

It is deeply unfair and unhelpful to castigate some of the less gifted entrepreneurs for their lack of forethought or presentation skills when the dragons have clearly been trained up for the show – having each spent hours in preparation and practice with professional TV coaches – are paid to appear on the programme and not infrequently take the opportunity to put down the people in front of them, in order to appear clever. Why can't they say, "Look, clearly you have spent a lot of time on this product/project, and with the right approach, it might work. Come and see me in my office next week, and I will give you half an hour of free advice, but I don't think you should take this to market – at least in its present form"?

In the early days of the programmes, it was noticeable that the norm for the dragons' investment was a company that had spent several years developing the product or service, then patented it, launched it, obtained and delivered significant orders, had more than a year of accounts showing an actual profit and can point to orders in the pipeline that assure profitability for many months or sometimes years ahead.

In other words, a no/low-risk, pretty well-guaranteed investment return – for which the dragons typically demand 30-40%, or more, of the share capital on the basis that their experience will be of help to the company, regardless of whether they personally know anything about that market!

Thankfully some of the entrepreneurs tell them to piss off, metaphorically speaking, and then the dragons look down their collective noses at them, finger the pile of (presumably) mock £50 notes beside each of them and have the nerve to say that the entrepreneurs should have accepted their help as they had made a good offer, implying that without them the entrepreneur will surely fail. Of course, some businesses succeed, though many fail – that's a given, but trampling on other people's dreams seems a cruel way to carry on.

And it is worth mentioning that even successful businesses are often only successful for a time until markets change, new products appear, or fashions fade. Who is to say that the dragons won't run into trouble themselves at some stage? Certainly, several have. The hubris shown by many, if not most, of them would indicate that nemesis is probably just around the corner.

It is noticeable that the pitches in recent years have tended to be for companies in the food and drinks sector, typically snacks, sauces and new flavours of gin or the like, rather than new innovative products that could find a market in the construction world, or as consumer electronics, for example. Does the world really need a new type of sauce? And how exactly do you make that unique and uncopyable?

Similarly, the responses from the dragons in recent years have tended to be more anodyne and less critical/sarcastic, with an occasional offer of entrepreneur mentoring. Interestingly, the equivalent programme on American TV – *Shark Tank* – still retains more of the original flavour of DD with new, invented products rather than snacks etc.

Funding – Apply... or Die!?

One of the most successful businessmen of the period between the World Wars, Tommy Sopwith, founder and head of Hawkers, when asked by a reporter what his recipe for success was, replied, "Luck, just luck". Can't you just see Peter or Deborah saying that? Well, no, not ever. Incidentally, Sopwith was one of the saviours of his country because when he was looking for powerful marine engines in the mid-1930s to drive his record-breaking powerboats (to win the Atlantic Blue Riband), he sent his chief engineer over to Germany to talk to the people at Dornier, who were a leading manufacturer of marine engines.

The engineer was taken round the Dornier plant by his engineering counterparts, who dismissed the marine engines and waxed lyrical about the secret aviation engines they were – in defiance of the Armistice terms – developing for heavy bombers. Sopwith's man came back to England and immediately told him what was going on. Sopwith, who was the main shareholder and managing director of Hawkers, promptly ordered the parts from suppliers for 1,000 Hurricanes – on his own cognisance and account, without waiting for an order from the Air Ministry.

The Hawker Hurricane bore most of the brunt of the Luftwaffe air assault in the Battle of Britain – accounting for over 60% of the Luftwaffe's losses, whereas the more famous Spitfire shot down about 40%. Without all the Hurricanes delivered before and during it, the Battle would certainly have been lost. Can you imagine a

Dragon ordering a thousand of **anything** on spec. to save his country if there was even the slightest risk to his own fortunes?

Government funding is regularly available through Innovate UK, and indeed, Hip Impact Protection (HIP) got some £50,000 of a grant directly from IUK in 2023 after submitting many proposals over the years. The unsuccessful bids were responded to by a panel of five 'experts', one of whom was enraptured by the idea, another would have preferred to eat shit rather than let it go through and raised every conceivable objection, often wanting more information on a topic such as "Market opportunity and exploitation plan" which would have been impossible to provide, in addition to the information actually included, (and approved by the other four experts) in the usual 400-word space provided.

The other three experts were generally warmly, or at least lukewarm, in favour of the proposal, but that did not sway the outcome. Apparently, this is typical, and although I have often complained to all and sundry, and outlier opinions are supposed to be discarded, the same thing happened time and time again. Interestingly, our successful bid was only reviewed by one person, so perhaps even IUK think their previous approach is flawed.

To show how fatuous the selection of suitable innovations is, I recall the SMART funding call, again from Innovate UK, that we participated in some time ago with the help of a consultancy that had had a good success rate in such calls. After considerable effort, we submitted a proposal for our ground-breaking technology, which was turned down, as usual. But to add insult to injury, the consultant told me that they had had success with a proposal from another company for a new earwax removal device!

Well, there are dozens of devices to remove earwax that are already on the market, and in any case, doctors love requests from patients for its removal as the procedure involves no costs to the practice since it uses a simple metal syringe from their cabinet and water, only takes a few minutes, is invariably successful and doesn't hurt the patient. What other medical procedure fits that bill?

Incidentally, I had had that problem and had purchased a set of hollow candle-type things that you lit and stuck in your ear and the suction drew out the earwax as the candle burned. My daughter had a boyfriend who had a blocked ear and tried to use this device. He nearly set fire to his hair but only loosened the earwax, so he used a cotton bud, which effectively rammed the earwax back in. He had to take several days off work as he couldn't hear anything until he got a doctor's appointment to remove it properly! My daughter 'moved on' soon after.

I also tried the Government's visa scheme whereby an intermediary company called InvestUK applied for us to the Home Office on behalf, in this case, of a doctor keen to relocate to the UK when he retired from his senior consultant position at a hospital in Riyadh. He was a very well-qualified gerontologist and had held senior positions at several hospitals in the UK over a nine-year period in the last century. He wanted to invest £150,000 in HIP to help it develop AI algorithms to predict falls using our Fall-Safe database and also act as a consultant for HIP. His knowledge of care for the elderly would have been invaluable to us.

You would have thought that, from every point of view, he would be an ideal candidate for this scheme, but the Home Office threw every possible objection in his way, delaying a decision that normally took a few months, for over a year, and finally rejected his application on totally spurious, incorrect and actually illegal grounds. We offered to fight the Home Office in court, but by that time, the good doctor had had enough and decided to retire to one of the Gulf States instead.

What an irony – the Home Office is only too happy to admit hundreds of thousands of un- or under-qualified people who the welfare state will probably have to support for years, not to mention all the people coming over illegally by boat, yet someone who would be readily assimilated into this country, could stand on his own two feet, and is prepared to make a substantial investment in a UK healthcare business, is prevented from doing so, illegally. But then the Home Office is taking its name so seriously that 50% of its staff are 'working' from their own homes!

A recent application to the National Institute for Health Research (NIHR) failed because they deferred to NICE and

Cochrane, who both published adverse reviews of hip protectors in about 2004 based on trials of such devices available in the 1990s.

NIHR pointed out that those reviews stated that hip protectors were only effective when worn in highly supervised nursing facilities and tended to cause pelvic fractures. I had already noted in my submitted proposal that these reviews referred to an earlier generation of hip protectors, which were hard shell devices to protect the hips made from polyethylene. Consequently, they were extremely uncomfortable to wear, so they would not be worn voluntarily, and transferred the impact force in a fall from the hip onto the pelvis. I had pointed out to NIHR that these devices had been discontinued many years ago and that, therefore the NICE and Cochrane reviews were very out-of-date and did not apply in present circumstances.

Nevertheless, NIHR were still not prepared to fund a trial of modern devices despite convincing evidence from a huge trial in Canada three years ago that found that, when worn, modern hip protectors prevented hip fracture and had no side effects. In what other medical field is evidence from a quarter of a century ago deemed still applicable and preferable to more recent evidence from trials?

Worse, if healthcare facilities are still taking such bad advice, elderly people susceptible to falls and fractures (since they have osteoporosis) are being placed unnecessarily at risk of hip fracture and, in 30% of such cases, mortality within one year. This is criminal negligence on the part of NIHR, NICE and Cochrane, and they should be prosecuted.

I intend to use the proceeds from the sales of this book to do just that. As the Dalai Lama said, "Our prime purpose in life is to help others, and if you can't help them, at least don't hurt them." Would that our much-vaunted healthcare authorities acted accordingly.

On Craftsmanship – How did you want to spend your life?

There is no doubt that the increasing use of computers has accelerated the dying arts of craftsmanship. Computer-Aided Design and Computer Aided Manufacture have frequently replaced the old manual skills of drawing and hand-making. While this has alleviated much of the drudgery of, for example, re-drawing architectural elevations and floor plans of buildings every time a change is made, it has de-skilled large numbers of the population and deprived them of the very real and enduring satisfaction to be gained from actually making something with their own hands.

Other than being paid large sums for sitting there in their dealing room or office using the telephone and computer screens, what satisfaction is to be gained from being an investment banker, for instance? As one wise and experienced banker once told me, "bankers don't actually **do** anything". Sure, some paper gets shuffled around and sent from place to place, but they are not actually **producing** anything for the vast sums they get paid – not earn, mind you.

And, it turns out, the taxpayer has to support them in this pastime because, apparently, almost any bank is now too large to be allowed to fail. Since human beings only learn not to do something by feeling pain, and bankers have really felt almost no pain after the last

(2007/08) crisis that they inflicted on the world economy by their excessive greed, we can be certain that a similar crisis will recur in the not-too-distant future.

There must only be limited job satisfaction from merely pushing paper around and taking telephone calls, don't you think? Are you going to be proud to say to your child or grandchild when they ask you what you did with your life, "Well, I sat in an office, made telephone calls – usually to other bankers – wrote on bits of paper, or used a keyboard and watched computer screens, that is when I wasn't sitting in meetings, or going to lunch"?

Would otherwise intelligent graduates from our top universities think that this is a worthwhile way to spend their working lives? To claim, as Lloyd Blankfein, the head of Goldman Sachs, one of the worst perpetrators of the global banking crisis, did, that they were just "doing God's work" is patently untrue, quite apart from the blasphemy involved.

Obviously, Blankfein just does not get it. The point is, for all the hours that they put in, will anyone remember, or care, what an investment banker (other than his/her own family) did the moment they left the firm or retired. It must be harder for a camel-hair-coated individual to pass through the eye of a needle than for an investment banker to enter the kingdom of heaven. If they had to pay the equivalent of VAT, i.e. 20%, as a transaction fee every time they wrote a deal, not only would there be far less exposure using complex mechanisms like Collateralised Debt Obligations, which no one properly understands, but the income generated would pay for the infrastructure that the UK badly needs.

(Incidentally, I was at a language school in Spain aged 18 with the man who later invented CDOs at Goldman Sachs, Robert E. Yaw II of Cedar Rapids, Iowa – you can imagine what his nickname was, at least among the English there!) But why should bankers not pay a transaction fee when everyone else does? It would also have the advantage that many of the Head Offices of the banks in the City would vacate London for other centres like Frankfurt, Paris or New York, and then those countries would be responsible for bailing them out in the next financial crisis.

As I said, bankers don't actually do anything, least of all help British industry, which was their original raison d'etre. Everyone knows that the City is not much more than a giant Ponzi scheme, forever trading forward – until, for some reason, the music stops – then they all fall off the roundabout... and the taxpayer picks up the tab – again.

Contrast bankers' life with that of a gunmaker I met several years ago. He had spent a lifetime making and repairing sporting shotguns as an independent and highly skilled craftsman. His work compares favourably with that of the output from the famous English gunmaker firms and he obviously derived enormous satisfaction from being one of the best, possibly the very best, man in his field worldwide. He had undertaken, at very low rates of pay, a long apprenticeship in order to learn his trade and had then proceeded to make sporting shotguns of every type which would be treasured by their owners for generations, ensuring that his name, Geoff Mobbs, inscribed on each gun, will be remembered with affection long after he is gone.

To make a top-quality gun, tailored personally for a customer, took him over 1,350 hours, and the result is not only visually stunning but beautifully balanced so it feels as light as a feather, is decorated with extraordinary scrollwork and, is not least, a mechanical masterpiece, designed and built to give good service to appreciative owners for hundreds of years. Anyone would be proud to own such a piece. Geoff Mobbs lived in a small house in Lincolnshire, and in fact his immaculate workshop next door had a floor area not much less than the house itself. He had earned the respect of everyone who knew him, not for merely being rich or famous like a banker but for the extraordinary and enduring quality of his craftsmanship.

My business partner, William Donelson, takes a similar view and his work, in this case, complex multimedia programmes, is still working without bugs ten or more years after he completed it. Indeed a young Frenchman recently contacted us as he said that our game *Foul Play* had changed his life and he was coming to England

and wanted to meet us. I replied that he might want to visit Holker Hall in Cumbria and see the actual rooms where we had filmed it.

I then sent him some visitors' vouchers I obtained from the staff at the Hall. He duly visited it last spring and wrote to me how much he had enjoyed it, even noting that he had found we had digitally reversed one of the rooms in order to fit it better into the virtual tour! Undoubtedly, there are some long-lived computer games, but they are in a small minority, and this standard of work is rarely seen in the world of computer software.

A notable characteristic of the true craftsman is that he or she is not particularly interested in seeking credit for his or her work, the quality of the work being a significant part of the reward. As Gandhi said, "My grandfather once told me that there were two kinds of people: those who do the work and those who take the credit. He told me to try to be in the first group; there was much less competition."

(Someone is bound to correct me here because, as we all know, the world is divided into two types of people – those who believe the world is divided into two types of people and those who don't). A good example of Gandhi's precept is the reaction of Tom Kilburn at Manchester University, who wrote the very first computer programme in the 1940s who, when he was asked whether he would write more programmes, replied that he had written one programme, and it had worked, so why would he want to write any more?

President Truman also observed, "It is amazing what you can accomplish if you do not care who gets the credit." The fact is that people who spend all their time seeking credit for some achievement, whether or not they actually deserve it, generally have no time to make further discoveries or developments. In the pop and rock music industry, for instance, there was a great deal of lobbying of the European Parliament to extend the copyright period from 50 to 70 years for songs performed and recorded by an artist – and that 70 years *starts* after the artist's death!

This is clearly ridiculous since it is not the performance of the song that is necessarily original but the writing of the song in the first place. Compare that with the relatively short period of patent protection of an invention, which expires after just 20 years. As usual, it is a question of who has more clout with the legislators, and it seems they are more concerned with protecting rock musicians, who have, to say the least, a doubtfully beneficial effect on society, than inventors whose work creates whole new industries employing masses of people.

It was notable that the musicians lobbying hardest for the change were of the likes of Paul McCartney and Cliff Richard, whose creative years are long behind them.

Finale & Credo

"If you can meet with triumph and disaster and treat those two impostors just the same..."

Recently, I discovered that Bill Gates, yes, the very same, had flown into London and been taken on a guided tour of Big Ben, the clock tower and bells, on its 150th anniversary. I hope he appreciated that clocks were the equivalent of computers in the 19th century and that the double three-legged gravity escapement invented by my great-great-uncle, Edmund Beckett-Denison, to control the huge clock hands and bells of Big Ben with the unprecedented accuracy of within one second a day, was the pinnacle of achievement in clock-making in that century.

Will people bother to lift a finger (to click a mouse button) to check out Mr Gates' achievements in 150 years' time? Will any of his systems run for 150 days (or even 150 hours), never mind 150 years, without crashing? In my experience, their Mean Time Between Failure is less than 150 minutes. The test of greatness is permanent public affection for your works.

Incidentally, Beckett-Denison's book "Clocks and Watches and Bells" became the standard work on those devices in the 19th century and contains far more advanced mathematics and algebra than I have ever found in any manual on computers or software – my ancestor had a First in Mathematics from Cambridge.

After a visit some years ago to Big Ben with nephews and nieces of all ages, I reflected on how to transport them back 150 years to understand the significance of the clock at that time. It occurred to me that it was really the super-computer of its day since it accepted, processed continually and disseminated – as widely as possible – a crucial piece of information, namely, the correct time.

Better-off people had their own personal devices, fob watches in their pocket, or mantelpiece and grandfather clocks at home, being equivalent to smartphones, laptops or desktops today, but there was no central service on which, at that time, they could rely, except Big Ben. Most people's first experience of computers some years ago was through 'Time Share' systems where the capacity of the system was shared with many users, who each got a piece of its facility in turn. Big Ben and all other timepieces of that period were undoubtedly single-purpose devices, but it could be said that even PCs are designed to be single-purpose systems – that purpose being the enrichment of Mr Gates through Microsoft.

Of course, one can only applaud the setting up and bountiful funding of their charitable organisation(s) by Mr & Mrs Gates (and separately since their divorce), with the proclaimed objective of using technological innovation to cure the world's ills – malaria for example, though releasing sterilised mosquitoes seems an improbable way of going about it – as if bug creation is not unknown to Mr Gates – but would it be uncharitable to question whether someone who set up a company which has enslaved millions of workers to what can be described as a technological freak show is really the right person to instigate and run such a project? I hope I am wrong, but experience indicates that top-down, throw-money-at-it approaches, such as the Gates' Foundation have adopted, rarely achieve the technological breakthroughs that they so eagerly anticipate.

Contrast their efforts with Leonard Cheshire VC and the most decorated pilot in World War Two, who subsequently founded the Leonard Cheshire Disability charity, which operates in 54 countries through over 250 independently managed organisations. He founded it in 1949 after taking a friend into his own home who was terminally ill with cancer. Or the Grameen Bank, which funds family-scale businesses in Third-World countries lending to the woman in the family, or the numerous small-scale projects like the sand dams or Warka Water in Africa. Bottom-up does work.

So, after a working lifetime of confronting the big battalions and making them pay for their misdeeds, what have I achieved? Well, certainly not riches or fame, and I have found that being lauded for your successes is nearly as uncomfortable as being denigrated for your failures because you almost always know that the praise is not fully earned nor deserved, just as the abuse usually isn't either.

Frequently, the person dishing out the plaudits does not really understand the hurdles overcome nor the route you have taken to overcome them, so at best, all I can usually manage is an embarrassed silence or – worse – self-effacing mumblings. I would emphasise that I have never gone out of my way to 'aggress' against anyone, and it has only been the frequently appalling and unethical behaviour of the large organisations with whom I have been obliged to deal that have caused me to react and take action against them. Should I have just laid down and let them roll over me? Probably, it would have been more profitable to do so, but I have always taken the same view as Thomas Watson of IBM: "If you stand up and be counted, from time to time, you may get yourself knocked down. But remember this: A man flattened by an opponent can get up again. A man flattened by conformity stays down for good." Thomas Watson was probably the greatest businessman of the 20th century.

Of course, it is certainly possible that my generally enthusiastic and cooperative attitude has led the various corporations, whom I have subsequently taken on and defeated, into the fallacy that I was too nice to mind if they tried to stuff me, and no doubt they have been surprised when I refused to lie down and roll over. Recent research has shown that trusting people has better mental health outcomes than trusting no-one.

I remember reading a business book by a successful American real estate broker in which he said that he had found there were three types of people in business. The first – and much the easiest to deal with – were the ones who made it absolutely clear up front, in one way or another, that when you reached for your chips, they would cut your arm off at the elbow if you gave them the opportunity. The second type were the ones who assured you that they would not cut you up but did so anyway.

The third type were the ones who went to great lengths to convince you that they were "straight kind of guys" and definitely would not, under any circumstances, cut you up – but still did so anyway. Publishers and most, but not all, charitable bodies like the Church and National Trust, in my experience, almost invariably fall into the third category and are consequently a nightmare to deal with. However, Ladbrokes, for example, fell into the first category.

My wonderful and beautiful daughter, Serena, when she was four, looked up at me one day and said, "What are people for, Daddy?" A pretty big question for a four-year-old or even a forty-year-old. In fact, if you think about it, the world's leading philosophers, academics, religious leaders, politicians, scientists, authors and historians have been working on and writing about, essentially this question for the past 4,000 years.

Well, I had roughly 20 seconds to come up with an answer if I was to retain that all-important credibility in my daughter's eyes. Obviously, it had to be short, understandable and hopefully memorable if the opportunity was not to pass. Fortunately, inspiration hit in time, and I replied, "To make other people happy". This satisfied her, and she went on playing. In the so-called "Selfish

Society" that we live in, perhaps it is not such a bad precept to live your life by – she certainly has. Would that the church preaches this message rather than concentrating on, or obsessing about, metaphysics, ritual, and side issues like women or homosexual priests and other baloney – when they are not engaging in politics? What do they know about Brexit? At least the Pope is, by definition, *allowed* to pontificate!

So, basically, life is not about you; it is about other people. Why is this concept so hard to grasp? As I wrote to my son Ralph, the successful racehorse trainer of many very good horses (not least *Bluestocking,* which recently won the Prix de l'Arc de Triomphe in Paris, Europe's richest and most prestigious race), when he was about to get married 20 years ago, "Life is not about a better house, a faster car, nicer and more exotic holidays or personal

aggrandisement, it is about your children and about the lady you are going to marry, who will look after and protect them" – or words to that effect.

There has been a fascinating long-term study begun in the late 1930s, called the Grant Research Project, directed by Professor Valliant at Harvard University for much of the past 72 years, which has regularly measured every aspect, physical and psychological, of a group of 268 men over that period in order to ascertain what makes people happy. Prof. Valliant sums up the conclusions by stating that "being nice" is the major component, defining happier people as those who place most emphasis on relationships and devote themselves to other people, especially loving spouses, children and grandchildren. He stated that people were happiest when they had determined to leave the world a better place than they had found it and spent their time doing things that had lasting value. I have tried.

To divert for a moment; proud as Virginia was, and I am, of Ralph's extraordinary achievements on the racetracks of Europe and America, it gave me especial pleasure that as President of the National Trainers Federation, he engineered a strike against the egregious proposal by the bookmakers to reduce the amount of money they provide to the Horserace Betting Levy for prize money. The strike involved ensuring that **no** horses were entered by trainers for three days of race meetings and also for individual races at Newbury and Lingfield. He was supported by a few notable trainers but encountered apathy or outright hostility from the majority of his contemporaries. However, Ralph is one of the few, possibly the only person to have successfully beaten the bookmakers, at least in recent times, perhaps ever.

When I was about 20, I went to Amsterdam – don't ask why – and visited the Rijksmuseum, where I encountered, for the first time, Vermeer's painting of *"The Woman in blue reading a Letter"*. It completely bowled me over and I felt certain that if there was a meaning to life, this was it. A few months later, I proposed to Virginia, my wonderful wife.

There have been many interpretations as to what Vermeer's picture means and who it represents, but it is now widely accepted that it was, in fact, one of Vermeer's daughters, pregnant (as with Leonardo's Mona Lisa) and therefore married. The reading of a letter symbolises love, and the inclusion of a map in the background indicates that the letter's writer is far away.

The fact that it was painted by Vermeer for the love, in his case of his daughter (as with Leonardo and his lover, the Mona Lisa) rather than to be sold or for a commission accentuates the warmth of the composition and brings the message home that life is ultimately about bringing children into the world, loving them and helping them to develop their potential. They then have their own children and look after those in turn, as you looked after them – what could possibly be more important than that? What else really do we leave behind? The point of the human race is survival.

Vermeer died in penury and left only about 35 paintings – and many of those were not commissioned. But his paintings are demonstrably the most widely loved and perhaps the most valuable ever produced – isn't that a legacy of love? Like all the greatest art, his paintings, just as Michelangelo's paintings and sculptures, tell us something about the human condition.

My favourite sculpture is Michelangelo's Madonna and Child in the Sint Salvador Cathedral at Bruges because her expression exactly mirrors that of my daughter, Serena, when she looked down at her (then) small son. Henry Moore's Madonna sculpture in St. Paul's Cathedral also has the same protective, loving feel to it. Art reflects real life and helps you to understand, and value it.

If that is not its true purpose, what is? In my case, the Vermeer gave me the rationale to ask Virginia to marry me at the now-unheard-of age of 21. How many people can say that the major decision of their life was taken because of a great work of art? As I had no money, no job – since I was leaving the Army shortly after we got married – no house to live in, a much-loved but deceased father, a very difficult (though very talented and determined) mother, no money, a poor education and not much in the way of prospects, I was no great catch, was I? So I needed all the assistance I could get, which I did by taking my love down to Mothecombe in South Devon to stay with old friends, the Mildmay-Whites.

Mothecombe is, to my, and many others', minds, perhaps the most beautiful place I know well on Earth – which I believe helped to persuade her to marry me; which she agreed to do on the way back from staying there in 1967.

But in some cases, if you have literally nothing to lose, press on. The only way of being certain about the success or otherwise of a prospective project is not to try it. As my father was fond of saying, "You can't be optimistic with a misty optic". I've never been exactly sure what he meant, but it seems to cover a multitude of sins. And let's face it, we are all sinners, aren't we – except my Virginia, who lived a blameless life. How many people can say that?

I have touched, jokingly, on the possibility of an afterlife, and as we get older this becomes a more pressing question than when one is in one's youth or even middle-age, and I pose this as an alternative to atheists and agnostics who do not believe in (or doubt) a deity and therefore the possibility of an existence, of some sort, after death. First, how can they be so sure when our knowledge of the universe is still – and probably always will be – so incomplete? As Isaac Newton, possibly the most brilliant man who ever lived, said, "Atheism is so senseless. When I look at the solar system, I see the earth at the right distance from the sun to receive the proper amounts of heat and light. This did not happen by chance". Is the average atheist smarter than Newton?

For the doubters' benefit I will retell two stories from two of the most pragmatic and observant men who you could ever hope to meet – if you were very lucky. First up is Jim Corbett, the famous hunter of man-eating tigers in the foothills of the Himalayas and hero of many such highly dangerous encounters, one of which particularly comes to mind. He had been pursuing a man-eater that had killed hundreds of people and one morning had gone out hunting for game for the pot with a light sporting rifle. He came upon a nullah or dried river bed and climbed down into it, though on his way noticed a nuthatch nest and took one of its eggs for his collection. He was holding it in his left hand so as not to break it, and, walking around a rocky outcrop in the bed of the nullah, he suddenly came face-to-face with the man-eating tiger crouching 20 feet away on the sandy riverbed. He said that he could have sworn that the tiger had a smile on its face at the very welcome arrival of what it thought would be its lunch.

Contrary to what you would think would be severe handicaps faced with the most dangerous animal on earth, there were three factors in Corbett's favour; first the fact that he had the nuthatch egg in one hand meant that he was not tempted to abruptly swing the rifle on to target the tiger – the natural thing to do and which would have immediately triggered the tiger's spring onto him before he could aim and fire, second that it was a light rifle that he could hold and control in one hand, whereas a proper rifle for shooting big game would have been far too heavy, and third the fact that he was facing a man-eater, because any other tiger would, as soon as it saw him, have immediately leapt forward and swept him aside in its desire not to be cornered. Being side-swiped by a tiger is usually fatal. So, he very gradually – and imperceptibly to the tiger – moved the rifle barrel the short distance to point at the tiger's throat (and spine

311

behind it) and fired. The tiger died instantly, and on examining it, he found that it was suffering from multiple shotgun pellet wounds in one shoulder that had gone septic and prevented it from hunting its normal prey. This would account for the moaning sound that villagers heard as it roamed around their houses at night, looking for prey. Corbett gratefully replaced the nuthatch egg back in its nest.

Jim Corbett, who uniquely has a major national park named after him in Northern India, recounts that, on another occasion, he was travelling on a track beside a steep and narrow gorge with a river running through it, when he was delayed by a rockfall and overtaken by nightfall and so had to camp where he was. During the night he saw hundreds of lights flicker on and off on the opposite side of the gorge and could not understand how that could happen as there was no electricity for many miles and no people around to carry torches. The next day he enquired at the next village as to what people made of this phenomenon. He was told that the path on the opposite side of the gorge had been a major pilgrimage route until some years before, when a flash flood had roared down the canyon and killed hundreds of pilgrims.

The second and equally dramatic story is recounted by William McRaven, retired four-star admiral and commander of the special forces that landed in Pakistan and found and killed Osama bin-Laden. His major contribution to the success of that mission was to insist that a back-up aircraft be ready to intervene if a helicopter crashed, as indeed happened. He had been a Navy SEAL (Special Forces) officer and, many years previously, had commanded an expedition to discover what had happened to a reconnaissance aircraft with seven crew on a training mission that had disappeared in the Rocky Mountains. There had been several reports from local inhabitants in succeeding years that something out of the ordinary was happening in the large crater of an extinct volcano that now held a substantial lake.

McRaven was put in charge of an exploratory expedition and landed in a helicopter on a little circular spur above the lake with a small force of SEALS equipped to dive or climb to find the aircraft. They realised that the lake's surface would have been frozen when the aircraft crashed in the late autumn and that it would have skidded onwards and hit the sides of the crater. There was only one place that the resulting debris would have not been apparent to search parties flying over the site, and that was below a glacier coming down one side of the crater wall. He decided to search the glacier by climbing up between the wall and the ice where there had been some melt and, therefore, the possibility of finding a route up it. They duly discovered some metal parts and also some small fragments of human bones and took these back to the camp for subsequent burial.

They had to wait until the next day to be helicoptered back to base, but during the night they all saw seven lights go slowly up from the lower edge of the glacier to the lip of the crater and then disappear. There was no electricity in the crater and no-one else there as the walls were near vertical.

You might say that there could be other explanations for these phenomena, but it seems more probable that these highly reliable and experienced observers reported exactly what they saw, as they had no interest in doing otherwise, and that these sightings are evidence of, at the very least, an alternative reality. Another view from Richard Feynman, the great physicist, who said, "I think I can safely say that no-one understands quantum mechanics". One of its phenomena being that a particle can be in two different places at the same time. Though it has been said that the human brain is perhaps the most extraordinary entity in the universe, it is apparent that despite incredible advances in scientific knowledge in the past 120-odd years – when my father was born (1891), it was ten years before the aeroplane had been invented, but when he died (1963) the space race was well underway – we do not even know how little we know.

You will have found many quotations in this book, though they are all from people pre-eminent in their fields, and one can only agree with Newton that it is possible to "see further by standing on the shoulders of giants". Appropriating and building on other people's wisdom has been responsible for most if not all, technological and scientific advances, and my hope for this book is that it will both encourage people to develop and use new technology for the benefit of mankind and most importantly, alert them to the likely opposition they will encounter en route so as to ensure they spend the time and effort to devise ways to surmount it, often involving others who may be able to help. If you are one of those technologists or inventors, the world needs you, and if not, don't stand in their way, nor stand back and throw rocks in their path.

Who knows whether Richard Branson (later Sir Richard) uttered the immortal words "Screw it, let's do it" when Mike Oldfield knocked on the door of his one-room office above a shop at the seedier end of Oxford Street in 1973 carrying a tape of his recording of Tubular Bells, a catchy hornpipe which he had created using one of the early 4-track overdubbing machines no less than 2,000 times. All Richard's experience of the music business had got him up to that point was a night in gaol and a £50,000 fine for VAT fraud exporting, importing and re-exporting records. Exactly what combination of Providence, persistence and luck brought the two together is impossible to say, but no one can dispute that Richard's innate marketing genius caused the rubber to hit the road at that point. Before that day, Mike Oldfield had been turned down by just about everyone of any significance in the music business, probably because they had never heard a music track like it. With no other options in sight for either of them, Richard leapt at it (or was so persuaded by his friend Simon Draper), but with 10 million sales, he was soon well down the road. Certainly, Richard has proved two things; first, that it is possible – no essential – to combine fun and profits to get right *Up The Organisation*, and second, that you are often, in business, obliged to *Kick Against the Pricks*!

As they say in Yorkshire, "Think on...."

In science, the credit goes to the man who convinces the world, not the man to whom the idea first occurs.

Sir Francis Darwin (1848 - 1925), Eugenics Review, April 1914

A life spent making mistakes is not only more honourable but more useful than a life spent doing nothing.

George Bernard Shaw

If history repeats itself, and the unexpected always happens, how incapable must Man be of learning from experience?

George Bernard Shaw

The man who writes about himself and his own time is the only man who writes about all people and all time.

George Bernard Shaw

If you don't make mistakes, you're not working on hard enough problems. And that's a big mistake.

Frank Wilczek - Physicist

It is not because things are difficult that we do not dare; it is because we do not dare that they are difficult.

Seneca

The man of virtue makes the difficulty to be overcome his first business and success only a subsequent consideration.

Confucius

It must be remembered that there is nothing more difficult to plan, more doubtful of success, nor more dangerous to manage than the creation of a new system. For the initiator has the enmity of all who would profit by the preservation of the old institutions and merely lukewarm defenders in those who would gain by the new ones.

Machiavelli

Your best shot at happiness, self-worth and personal satisfaction – the things that constitute real success – is not in earning as much as you can but in performing as well as you can, something that you consider worthwhile.

William Raspberry

My Motivation?

We all like to think that our parents and ancestors would approve of our achievements, great or small, as being consonant with their own approach to life, so it might be illuminating to look back at the backstory of members of the Beckett family since the Victorian era, and this will perhaps indicate why I have taken paths throughout my life that were intended primarily to benefit others just as they had, rather than, to a much lesser extent, myself and my family.

- **Edmund Beckett Denison, first Lord Grimthorpe** 1816 - 1905 (my great, great uncle). Notable lawyer with a connection to the Great Northern Railway, which built a line from York to London – still probably the most successful railway line in the country. He designed the Westminster Clock, inventing the special escapement mechanism which drives the huge hands on the world famous clock face and the bells and Big Ben. It operates in all weathers and is accurate to 2 seconds a week. This was unprecedented. He undertook this task without payment, as well as those of designing the clock for Big Tom at St. Paul's Cathedral and 100 or so turret and church clocks around the country.

My Motivation?

- **The second Lord Grimthorpe**, 1856 - 1917 (my grandfather), MP and patron of Auguste Rodin, to whom he suggested that the sculpture of *The Thinker* be scaled up from the tiny figure created for Rodin's *Gates of Hell*. My grandfather commissioned a bust of Eve Fairfax, his fiancée, from Rodin before the latter's seduction of Miss Fairfax caused him to break off the engagement. He bought and developed the house and gardens at Cimbrone, near Amalfi in Southern Italy, one of the most spectacularly beautiful gardens in that country. He, therefore, was partially or largely responsible for the creation of no less than three masterpieces – how many people can say that? He sold his house and 430-acre estate in Leeds, Kirkstall Grange, latterly Beckett Park, for a nominal amount to Leeds Corporation in 1917, which used it to help create Leeds Beckett University, now educating 36,000 students.

- **The third Lord Grimthorpe**, 1891 - 1963 (my father), joined the Royal Flying Corps in 1917 and was a leading sportsman after the Great War, winning the Curzon Cup on the Cresta Run and over 50 point-to-point horse races. He funded the start-up of the Airspeed Company with Nevil Shute Norway (production engineer and latterly author) and A. H. Tiltman, designer, in 1931 to build aeroplanes in York. He had had the opportunity of buying 2,000 acres adjacent to his house near Castle Howard for only £10 an acre, but in the Depression, he knew that this would only employ relatively few people, whereas he expected Airspeed to employ over 100 people in York, as indeed it duly did. With the assistance of (Sir) Alan Cobham, the company pioneered in-flight refuelling and developed the first production retractable undercarriage. This latter was demonstrated to Arthur Mitchell and Sydney Camm, with representatives of the Air Ministry in the mid-1930s. Camm was reluctant to incorporate it into his design of the Hurricane until he was told the Air

319

Ministry would not order his aircraft without it since it improved performance by about 15%. Would the Battle of Britain, which was such a close-run thing, have worked out as well without it?

Airspeed was eventually acquired by the de Havilland aircraft company in June 1940, and its most successful design, the Envoy, was converted into a 2-engined trainer for bomber crews, the AS.10 Oxford, with over 8,500 machines built during the war (apart from the DC3, the then largest civilian aircraft production run). Airspeed also manufactured 3,700 Horsa assault gliders, which were used on D-Day, at Arnhem and in the Rhine crossing assault. Post-war, Airspeed went on to produce the superbly streamlined, pressurised twin-engined piston airliner called the AS57 Ambassador. This served successfully for some years with British European Airways as their elite "Elizabethan Class". Finally, Airspeed was merged into de Havilland.

- **Count Manfred Beckett-Czernin** DSO, MC, DFC 1913 - 1962 (my first cousin) was one of "The Few" in the Battle of Britain, shooting down 19 enemy aircraft before being shot down himself by no less a German ace than Adolf Galland. He was awarded the DSO and DFC for his bravery during the Battle. As he spoke perfect Italian and German, he was recruited by Special Operations to parachute into Northern Italy in mid-1944 in order to set up a partisan network. After twice getting mixed torchlight signals from the ground, on his own initiative, he elected to jump anyway and, fortunately, was received by the partisans. He was awarded the MC for jumping so courageously into the blue. He duly set up a very effective partisan network.

Some months later, he was picked up and returned to Allied lines but volunteered to be parachuted once more into Northern Italy to organise partisan resistance in March 1945. After innumerable hardships and dangers, he managed, with a few partisans, to meet the German General commanding an important sector and persuaded him to surrender his 3,000-strong force to the partisans. He had driven to meet the general in a Fiat saloon car with the Union Jack painted on the bonnet! A German 88mm anti-aircraft gun was trained on it on the way as they passed an airfield, but for some reason did not open fire. The Italians believe that his initiative saved over 2,000 lives and prevented enormous damage to the towns and infrastructure in that sector.

So, it would hardly be surprising if I felt obliged by such a family history to make every effort to try to improve the world through what I knew best, the application of technology by attempting to fix obvious problems as I saw them in healthcare, education, quality standards in industry, control of trading (and traders) in the City, desk-to-desk communications (email), non-violent deductive games, industrial and military training and recruiting and much else. The family motto is, after all, *"Prodesse civibus"* or "For the good of the people".

In most, if not all, of these areas, it was apparent that no one else was going to tackle the task, so why not me? I take the view that it is no use carping about the state of play in any particular area of interest; you actually have to demonstrate, with a viable product, that it can be done otherwise. I have also taken the view that the product has to be as perfect as you can make it so that it does not get rejected by the user, and to date (apart from a few ingrates with spurious complaints), I and my associates believe that we have never had any products rejected for valid reasons. Can Bill Gates or Microsoft (since he left) say that? If you are not producing an excellent product, it will not be fun and profitable, and if it's not, why the hell are you doing it?

To see many of the products that I and my partners have produced, please visit:

www.armchair-travel.com

It may seem unbelievable that a tiny outfit like Armchair Travel Ltd., with just two guys, assisted by two or three freelance, though dedicated, helpers, could create all those extraordinary and visually arresting programmes and products in just a few years. Products which I am told have been seen and used by tens of millions of people all over the world – but really, it happened.

For my more recent work, see:

www.hips-protect.com

Printed in Dunstable, United Kingdom